Why Divide When You Can Multiply?
Sow A Seed - Feed A Nation

Robert A. Needham, JD
with Pastor Mark Schrade, MDiv

Title: Why Divide When You Can Multiply?
SubTitle: Sow A Seed – Feed A Nation

Printed in the United States of America

ISBN: 978-0-9837372-4-7
Cover Design: Renee Howard

Contact the Authors: www.wdwycm.com

Contents

Dedication

Our book is dedicated to all the marketplace leaders and ministry innovators who are diligently developing strategies, plans and structures to accomplish God's Mandates in their lives. This new breed of social entrepreneurs, form a network of change agents that are preparing a remnant for the soon return of Jesus Christ. For those involved in Kingdom Economics, we pray this book will help equip you for a life sacrificial service.

The authors acknowledge the sacrifices of their families who provided the grace to enable them to invest the time in writing this book.

Acknowledgments

We would like to thank **William S. Bojan, Jr.**, CEO and Founder of Integrated Governance Solutions and **Jim Weiland**, Director, Market Development for contributing in the area of governance expertise. We encourage you to learn more about their company and software called Solomon 365 at www.solomon365.com and www.integratedgovernance. com.

We would like to thank **Neil F. Garfield, JD, MBA** for his contributions and insight in the area of the global mortgage crisis. Neil and his team of dedicated anti-foreclosure experts are making a meaningful difference in the plight of millions of American consumers. Neil is an accomplished attorney, author, blogger, and entrepreneur. We encourage you to join his more than 6,300,000 readers of LivingLies Blog at livinglies.wordpress. com or www.AmericanHomeOwnersCoOp.com.

We would like to thank **David Auterson, CFRM** for his contributions and research in the area of marketplace ministry, earned-income strategies, and ministry funding. David is a nationally recognized expert in his field. You may contact David through this book's website at www.wdwycm.com.

We would like to thank **Cheryl-Ann Needham**, **M.Ed.** for her contributions to this work, prophetic revelation, and intercessory prayer covering. Cheryl-Ann is a ministry and business advisor to marketplace leaders as well as an author. You can learn more about Cheryl-Ann by visiting her website at www.cheryl-ann.com.

We would like to thank **Bruce Cook, PhD.** for his encouragement and support of Kingdom Economics and his Forward to our book. Dr. Cook is Apostle, Author, and the Convener of the Kingdom Economic

Yearly Summit (K.E.Y.S.). You can learn more about Dr. Cook and how to participate in this excellent networking conference at www. kingdomeconomicsummit.com.

Endorsements

As an "avid adversary" of all things Babylonian, I can truly appreciate Dr. Needham's powerful new book **"Why Divide When You Can Multiply? Sow a Seed – Feed a Nation."** This book helps to diagnose, diffuse and destroy some of the Babylonian culture's greatest strategies; those which have crippled not only how our financial systems work, but how our lives are shaped as a result.

Reading this work left me not only informed but interested. Dr. Needham is clearly an "apostle of acquisition" and carries a mandate for the re-education of our financial mentality. His principles for reformation and recovery are profound. These ground level revelations are practical yet they reflect heaven's best, giving us a supernatural opportunity for change.

"My people are destroyed for lack of knowledge: because thou hast rejected knowledge, I will also reject thee, that thou shalt be no priest to me: seeing thou hast forgotten the law of thy God, I will also forget thy children." Hosea 4:6

Dr. Needham's book is filled with truth that produces knowledge and we'll do well to learn from it. He has addressed the importance of natural and spiritual laws and how they relate to the success of our generation and those to come. This will become one of the handbooks that we'll be using to educate and transform our generations!

Dr. Gordon E. Bradshaw
Author - *Authority for Assignment – Releasing the Mantle of God's Government in the Marketplace*
President / Governing Apostle – *Global Effect Movers & Shakers Network* (GEMS)
Senior Scholar of Spiritual Formation and Leadership – Hope Bible Institute & Seminary
www.GEMSNETWORK.org
Chicago, Illinois

Straight from the heart of God, in the Book of Genesis, comes the profound revelation that ***Multiplication*** is His Supernatural Method to spread His blessings around the world. For far too long both the marketplace and the church have used simple ***Addition*** as the primary principle of growth. If we catch the revelation Robert Needham unfolds in this book, with the Biblical methods of multiplication, it will dramatically change our lives. The author's perspective about the actual distinctions between the existing ***Babylonian Economic System*** and the emerging ***Kingdom Economic System*** are revealed in a way that every believer will understand. Robert's picture of ***Convergence*** is one you should frame and put on the wall of your office so you can always remember who you are and where you are going. In the last few years, the Lord told me to make sure I was in the right stream and to exhort others to get in the right alignment with the Lord, the right calling and the right associates. I encourage you to read this book and follow its revelations. I heartily endorse Robert Needham, Mark Schrade, and their work.

Duncan Campbell,
Apostolic Missionary and Equipper
Co-Founder of Joy Ministry and Kingdom Marketplace, LLC
President of Kingsway Consultants & Investors
and Associated Brokers Co.
DuncanandWendy.com
Fayetteville, Arkansas

Why Divide When You Can Multiply?, is a definition, history and "Mapquest" of the U.S. economic and political systems and structures and why they are failing. It is also a roadmap out of the limited confines of the world's systems and through the doorway of convergence into the unlimited Kingdom systems and perspective.

Fulton Sheen
CEO of Merging Streams Commonwealth
Director of Isaiah 58:12

Talk about thinking outside the box! I found Robert's book to offer intriguing perspectives, persuasive arguments, powerful principles and provocative prospects.

Tim Taylor
An apostle & Commander, USNR-retAuthor, Speaker, Strategic ConsultantFounder of Kingdom League International
www.KingdomLeague.org
Renton, WA

Why Divide When You Can Multiply?, is a great guideline for your future. It doesn't matter if you are a business man or woman, in the largest or smallest city, or the Bishop of hundreds of churches, you will want to have this book in your library. Dr. Needham uses his personal story and experience to reveal some amazing truths about how God's plan for you, no matter your story, or where you came from, it is guaranteed to happen. Once you start reading, you will not be able to put it down.

Jamie Tuttle
Lead Pastor
Dwelling Place Church International
Cleveland, TN

The systems of this world seek to possess, acquire, and control the very people it is supposed to serve. This book takes you on a journey of exposure to the systems that have never worked, and that never will work, and toward the only solution there is, Christ and His Kingdom. Dr. Robert Needham brilliantly uncovers the lies we have believed while pointing to the only real solution and that is to unite the streams of faith to produce rivers of abundance and glory to our God. This is revelational and reformational insight that I highly recommend.

Robert Ricciardelli
Founder
Converging Zone Network
Belleview, WA

In his latest book, Robert Needham lays out a simple but extremely powerful and compelling collaborative faith based pathway that at the end of which any ministry will be on their way to financial self-sufficiency. Robert has seen a lot between his many entrepreneurial business endeavors, Christian faith and service, personal challenges, and unrelenting mission to share knowledge for the betterment of others. He understands history, changing economic tides, and the blessings that come to the faithful. Robert's clear and concise new economic order based upon collaboratively harnessing personal networks and circles unleashes true economic power to the faithful. Read this book and prosper!

Alex H. Cunningham
CEO FranCnsult
Lexington, Kentucky

Dr. Needham is considered a franchise development innovator and expert. His book *Solving the Puzzle of Owning a Franchise* was a huge hit in franchise industry. Now, in his 14th book, Robert is taking his more than 25 years experience as a franchise and business consultant and innovating in the area of cooperatives. I find his thoughts on Fourth Sector business strategies refreshing.

In this new book, *Why Divide When You Can Multiply?*, he truly takes a look at the current world situation and his proposal for a parallel Kingdom Economic System to ultimately replace a failing world economic system is timely!

I strongly recommend this as a must read for all business and ministry leaders alike.

Lonnie Helgerson, CFE
CEO Helgerson Franchise Group
Author, *5 Pennies: Ten Rules to Successfully Building a Franchise Mega-Brand and Maximizing System* Profits
Orlando, Florida

The title sums up the message: Why would we shrink what God has made limitless? Why settle for less when God has provided for more? But the answers to these questions will surprise you. This is no rehash of the "American Dream" nor is it the "prosperity gospel" explained another way. Rather, the ideas in this book provide groundbreaking approaches to understanding Kingdom Economics, by which I mean economics that glorify the King! Just as the explosive growth of house church movements world-wide has shown the church "why divide when you can multiply!", so this book explains why it is that business thrives when it is built on Biblical precepts of mutual sharing (Cooperatives), gleaning (giving to the poor) and seed sowing (the inherent power of anything God gives us to multiply indefinitely). Rather than fractional returns (5%, 15% or "hyper-growth" at 50% per annum), is it possible to see multiplied growth (5 fold, or 15 fold or even 100 fold). God word says "Yes!" and this book stands solidly on God's word!

Dr. Tony Dale
Founder and Chairman of the Board of The Karis Group
former President and Co-Founder of House2House Ministries.

Foreword

Why Divide When You Can Multiply? by my good friend and marketplace colleague, Dr. Robert Needham, is both a probing and profound question, and one that deserves an honest and sincere answer. Each of us should take this question to heart, pray about it, receive wisdom and strategy for it, and answer it in our own way as a matter of biblical stewardship and son-ship. Dr. Needham, from his vast and varied background as a rocket scientist, engineer, business consultant, author, entrepreneur, CEO, and attorney, has shared in this book his wisdom and God's revelation for this season that is both practical and applicable, as well as theoretical.

We know from nature and from agronomy, biology, chemistry, zoology, economics, physics, and other sciences, that multiplication is the way of life, the path of increase, and the fruit of economic empowerment that God has designed. Yet, far too often we stop to realize that the prerequisite to multiplication is death. John 12:24 (NIV) says, "I tell you the truth, unless a kernel of wheat falls to the ground and dies, it remains only a single seed. But if it dies, it produces many seeds". You and I are the kernel of wheat in this parable in a spiritual sense, and we must die to the fleshly, carnal nature and even to our own will, understanding, thoughts, ideas, desires, and dreams at times. According to Matthew 6:33, "seek first his kingdom and his righteousness and all these other things will be given to you as well," then spiritual germination can occur in our hearts and minds, with the result that we "…are being transformed into His likeness with ever-increasing glory" (2 Cor. 3:18), and are being "transformed by the renewing of your mind" (Rom. 12:2).

The nature of God's Kingdom and Word, as reflected in the Law of Multiplication, is that they are ever-increasing, ever-expanding, ever-effective, ever-fruitful, ever-potent, ever-powerful, and everlasting. When we focus on ourselves and our own finite resources, we limit ourselves and have either an ownership and prideful mentality and attitude, or one of poverty and entitlement/welfare, depending on our resources, circumstances, and/or identities. Only when we focus on God and His unlimited, infinite resources, then we are empowered to grow, change, mature, receive discipline and refinement, form covenant relationships, be transformed and become more like him, be properly aligned with others and with God, and to access His resources as we co-labor and co-create with Him as sons and daughters of the Most High.

Dr. Needham has succinctly and successfully translated timeless truths, eternal laws, and principles into the pages of this book for us to learn, profit, and benefit. Chapter 8 alone on the concept and function of a Collaborative Commonwealth is worth the price of the book; everything else is a bonus. I highly recommend this book and its author to you and encourage you to begin multiplying and stop dividing today.

Dr. Bruce Cook
Austin, Texas

Preface

I want to thank you for your decision to read this book. I truly hope it will bless you as it has Pastor Mark Schrade and me to write it. We are providing you this overview so that you will understand the flow of this book and how to get the most out of it.

When I was in government, they always said when you are making a presentation you need to 1) tell them what you are going to tell them (the overview), 2) tell them (the book itself), and 3) tell them what you have told them (our last section called Conclusions).

As God gave me the chapters of this book, I knew it was to be written first to marketplace leaders and second to church leadership. I feel that God has prepared me to write to business people. As a business consultant and strategic advisor to business now for almost 25 years, I have worked in more than 90 industry segments and helped develop over 300 business concepts. I often tell my clients, "What is the best way to choose a consultant or advisor?" The answer is simple, "Choose the one who has made the most mistakes! That consultant or advisor knows where the pot holes and dangers are, not just theory of how business works." Certainly I must confess I am greatly qualified based on failure.

I remember in May of 2010, Tom Crawford, at that time was a consultant with the Church Extension Plan, and I were having breakfast in Mountainbrook (near Birmingham). Tom had flown into town to meet with me at the request of a dear friend of mine, David Auterson who was with the Assemblies of God church planting team, The Church Multiplication Network. David had shared a White Paper I had authored in November 2009 entitled *The Concept Management Company (CMC)*. This is how David and I met, by a divine appointment facilitated by David Lisi (his brother in law) and president of Life and Homes Magazine (a franchise concept I had developed earlier that year). Now another divine appointment would take place with Tom as he would learn what I was about, but as important, Tom would provide me a prophetic word. That day, Tom, a man I just met, delay his second meeting to give me a word, that he did not even understand; but when I heard it, it would lead me to my Convergence. Tom simply said, "I don't understand this, but God wants me to tell you that 'when you see your ships burning, don't be concerned I am just getting the distractions out of your way'." What Tom did not know was that I referred to businesses I start as ships. In fact, I have instructed thousands of business students that as an entrepreneur your must constantly be launching ships (new ideas) and that if you launch 10 in a year, 8 will surely sink (fail) and the last 2 will return with treasure (make a profit), unless there are pirates. And there are often pirates. Failure is how entrepreneurs temper their steel. Within the next 12 months, every business deal I was in would either terminate or be shaken as God aggressively nudged me into my ministry!

As I shared this story with my pastor, Mark Schrade, who understands the essential need to merge the gifts of kings and priests through marketplace ministry, he shared with me Dr. Clinton's model of *Leadership Emergence Concepts* and how I was entering into my Convergence. Over the next few months as God clearly told me to write this book, Mark would be there for me all the way as my guide. I could think of no one more qualified to add the biblical research for this book than Mark. He is my Pastor. In his former assignment he fully integrated marketplace ministry and community development in West Virginia in a very depressed area. Mark is on numerous boards and is a staunch Biblicist.

In Daniel 11:32-33, we find prophesy of our "assignment" for these end times:

32 Those who do wickedly against the covenant he shall corrupt with flattery; but the people who know their God shall be strong, and carry out great exploits. 33 And those of the people who understand shall instruct many; yet for many days they shall fall by sword and flame, by captivity and plundering. New King James Version

In these two verses is the state of the world today and our mandate (response). First we are told that "32 those who do wickedly against the covenant, he will corrupt with flattery;" (Satan and his organizations). This is the state of the world today. We are seeing terms such as Globalization and the New World Order which are synonyms of a One World Government in the making and Satan flatters them with the "good" it will do. We are also seeing the emergence of a blending of religions, like "Chrislam", believing that there is more than one way to heaven and that faiths can merge like Christianity and Islam. This form of deception is causing noted, so called, Christian leaders to convene and support such false doctrine flattering them as seeking peace in direct contradiction of scripture. Have you ever heard that when a person speaks to you followed by a "but", the real message follows the "but". So here in verse 32, we have that "; but the people who know their God (this should be you) shall (a command, not a suggestion) be strong and carry out great exploits." (Your calling) [Emphasis added (…)]. Also when such a thought is followed by an "And" it further clarifies. "And those of the people who understand (their calling) shall instruct many." (Make disciples). So this is why we wrote this book, to "instruct many" knowing that there is a promise of criticism and more "yet for many days they shall fall by sword and flame, by captivity and plundering." (it will not be easy!).

I must admit that the book I began is not the book we finished. In 2010, I was at World Net Daily's conference before they departed for the "Tea Party At Sea." I was invited by Michael O'Fallon, president of Sovereign Cruises and Events to have a booth there to introduce Kingdom CoOp. As God would have it, one of Mike's Constitutional

Panel would become ill and at the last minute, I would get the opportunity to sit on the illustrious panel before thousands in attendance and on TV.

I immediately texted several pastors and intercessors, who pray for me, and asked if they would pray that I would get asked the one right question to bring honor to God. I did, it was the last question asked of this notable panel. A young man asked, "President Obama often cites the Sermon on the Mount as his biblical reference for how he wants to fix the economy – by dividing the wealth. Using the same reference, explain why he is wrong!" I immediately knew this was my question. I raised my hand and said, "That the Feeding of the 5000, during the sermon, if you understand it, was not about "dividing the wealth" (loafs and fishes), it was about multiplying Kingdom resources." Then I said, "it is simple… Why Divide When You Can Multiply?" You could have heard a pin drop all over the convention. God had given me the title for my next book.

My first thoughts were to write on some sexy Kingdom Marketplace Strategies using the power of cooperatives and the CMC. As I began to write, God changed that, ask me to add Pastor Mark Schrade as a co-author and Biblicist to comment on these ideas, and gave me **three distinct movements**. They are:

Movement 1: The current state of people, government, and the World Economic System (division). Chapters 1 – 5.

Movement 2: Kingdom Economics, cooperatives and multiplication principles and strategies. Chapters 6 – 9.

Movement 3: Plan B – Transition into the Millennial Kingdom. Chapters 10 – 12.

Movement 1 speaks to God's call and favor leading to a mandate (a Convergence – Chapter 1). How Crisis, is used by a "power elite" to manipulate and distract us. That our concept of wealth and freedom has been corrupted by Mammon's plan of World Economics based in Division. For us to clearly see Satan's deception of how central power has corrupted three sectors: 1) Public (Government/Governance), 2) Private (Business), and 3) Social (non-profits), and has led to corruption in the Modern Church by its falling into a similar pattern of central control and a rebellion by its members made manifest in their GIVING being in significant decline.

We considered the 40 and 80 year economic cycles and found that in United States we are seeing a very predictable repeat of the Great Depression caused by certain failed financial concepts like a Central Bank and a debt-based currency which have been used by Satan as a lever to enslave and move us toward his ultimate plan of a One World Government and Economy as our only option.

Movement 2. Starting in Chapter 6, we introduce why God's Kingdom Economic System which returns power and wealth to many, instead of Satan's power elite. We discuss how that Faith without Works is Dead. We understand God's multiplication power, Sow A Seed – Feed A Nation! By using "Multiplied Giving" as our weapon we can defeat Satan's plan based in division and debt (greed). We simply call it as be see it – To leave Babylonian concepts governed by a power elite and move toward a concept called "Collaborative Commonwealth" that will lead God's people out of Babylonian Captivity (debt), through the wilderness of the Tribulation ahead, into a Promised Land (the Millennial Kingdom).

Movement 3. In Chapters 10 – 12 we ask the hard question, "Do we need another system?" We present three scenarios for you to consider. We clearly state as Christians and Americans that we can no longer believe the lie "that divided we stand and united we fall."

We propose a Transition "Plan B" as a parallel alternative to a failed world system. We challenge individuals (Drops) to join with like-mined social networks/circles we call Streams. We encourage Streams to unite (merge) with other Streams to form Rivers (movements with power) all moving toward the Ocean (a promised land – the Millennial Kingdom).

All this to say, there is HOPE in Occupying the Promises of God and not being enslaved by a system of central power and a failed World Economic System. Our book is bold, it is controversial, and it calls for REFORMATION not revolution!

We pray we see you at the Ocean!

Vision & Prophecy:

5 Stages of the Kingdom Economic Governance System

September 2011

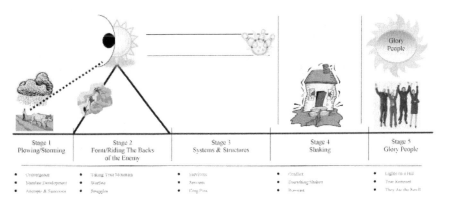

Stage 1 Plowing/Storming	Stage 2 Form/Riding The Backs of the Enemy	Stage 3 Systems & Structures	Stage 4 Shaking	Stage 5 Glory People
• Convergence • Mandate Development • Attempts & Successes	• Taking True Mountain • Warfare • Struggles	• Interviews • Servants • Emp Pres	• Conflict • Everything Shaken • Remnant	• Lights on a Hill • True Remnant • They Are the Sew'd

I, Cheryl-Ann Needham, in the Spirit, saw the Lord began to draw as if on a whiteboard what I will refer to as our next Five Stages of a Kingdom Economic Governance System. Here is the description of the vision as well as the explanation I heard from the Lord written through mostly my voice.

5 Stages = "Grace"

The vision included five distinct stages. He brought to my remembrance that the number five in the Bible represents grace and elaborated that He is providing a way to secure provision and funding for many. Not all will participate in the establishment of these systems, but all can benefit.

Stage 1 – Plowing/Storming

During this stage, I saw individuals (who I will refer to as Stewards) plowing a field. Each Steward had been entrusted with a particular part of the Lord's Kingdom Economic Government System; which was represented by his or her Kingdom Mandate. Each Steward was using a plow share, a cutting device attached to the plow itself that enabled the Steward to tread ground in an efficient manner.

The work was long and laborious as much plowing and sowing needed to be done. Because the territory was unfamiliar, each Steward had to keep his or her eyes on the sun (i.e. "Son") in order to know how and where to plow. As each looked to the Son, the respective path was made clear for the plowing and sowing. In the diagram, this is indicated by the line going up to the sun (Son) as well as the line coming back to indicate to the Steward where to plow next.

I heard the Lord say, "A government is to SERVE the people it represents. Jesus Christ SERVED. Ultimately, these individuals will have to be servants of many." He continued, "I do not show favorites and I do not favor a son or daughter above an individual who is not. My Love goes out to all unequivocally. A Steward is not only responsible to bring a new structure or approach to the millennial reign, but to win as many as possible on his or her way up the mountain."

This stage was also marked by a "storming" affect in that there were two forms of conflict each Kingdom Mandate Steward needed to resolve. The first conflict had to do with the Mandate itself. Significant questions related to the specific nature of the Mandate, its target, and end result needed to be resolved. For many, the path to plow consisted of several twists and turns as each pursued clarity for his or her Kingdom Mandate. The second source of conflict was regarding the issue of relationships; specifically who should help and how? Since each Kingdom Mandate Steward was in completely new territory and doing something much greater than he or she could ever do alone, many questions needed to be resolved. Hence this stage felt like navigating through a storm.

I heard Him say, "Only a select few will be positioned and prepared to put their hands to the plow. Those who have been called and positioned have already been doing it. These laborers must be servants of all or they will not be servants of any. Although each Steward has a tendency to have tunnel-vision because of the specialty of focus, each and every person's heart will need to be enlarged so that a love for every single person on earth is present. This is not time to distinguish between the haves and the have-nots, believers and unbelievers. It ain't over until I say its over and I say it ain't over. So do not presume you know who is in which camp."

Stage 2 – Form/Riding the Backs of the Enemies

Stage 2 was marked by each of the Stewards climbing up the left side of a large mountain that was indicated in the vision as a triangle. The key word for this stage was *Form*. During this stage, the Kingdom Mandates had sufficiently formed, having taken shape with a clear vision and destination target for each. The clarity was a significant relief to those who had plowed almost in the dark in the previous stage.

The climb up the mountain was significant as the mountain itself represented the enemy's counterfeit economic system. Each Steward was entrusted with a specific strategy to literally "ride the backs of the enemies" to the top of the mountain. These secret strategies would be unique to each Kingdom Mandate. Yet all will arrive at the same place ready for launch. Some will ride the backs of their enemies in plain sight; others will be hidden.

On the top of the triangle was a circle that in conjunction with the triangle bore a striking resemblance to the symbol on our dollar bill. During this phase, secrecy is of utmost importance. Many Stewards will be entrenched with the enemy in ways they've never been before and this will be for a strategic positioning as in the stories of Daniel and Joseph. The strategies of the Lord for each Steward will NOT be plain for others to see or understand so misunderstandings can occur.

The Kingdom Mandate entrusted to each Steward was represented by a boulder about four feet in diameter. Each Steward was carrying his or her "boulder" up the mountain. There was "weightiness" to the climb given the upward slope of the mountain as well as the heaviness of the Mandate itself. The struggle and warfare became more and more intense as each Steward neared the top.

The goal of each Steward was to get to the circle at the top of the mountain. The circle represented the "Eye of the Storm" where the Stage 3 would begin. At this point, I could see part of the eye of the storm become a pupil in the Lord's eye. His eye transcended the evil eye and even used it for His purpose! (See diagram).

Stage 3 – Systems and Structures

Stage 3 consisted of the launching of new *Systems and Structures* from the Eye of the Storms. There were two parallel lines coming out horizontally from the circle at the top of the mountain which had three explanations. First, the parallel lines represented a parallel economic governance system. Second, they represented the boundaries of a river with multiple streams (or Mandates) coming together and comprising the entire river. Third, they represented a bowling alley. At the end of the bowling alley were 3 "kingpins" which represented sources of demonic stronghold. The boulder shaped Mandates were to be thrust down the bowling alley knocking down the kingpins. A kingpin is the particular pin in bowling that when struck properly, causes the other nine pins to drop. To strike a kingpin is a big deal!

The Kingdom Mandates are to be released like a bowling ball, each in successive order and fashion. The timing of each Mandate's release is critical; each serving as a weapon in its own right. This launch of new Systems and Structures will be a total affront to the enemy and a time when "all hell will break loose". At this point, the Lord reminded me of the attack against Pearl Harbor. A few U.S. planes were able to get air borne but they were flying against hundreds of Japanese planes. The onslaught of the enemy during this stage will be similar to that level of warfare.

He assured however, that there will be a supernatural empowering similar to the days of Israel and her many God-made victories. In fact, at this point He gave me a vision of a scene in the movie <u>King Kong</u> where he climbed the Empire State Building. Although planes swirled around attacking King Kong, he batted them away like flies. The Lord assured, "The miracles these Stewards' witness to launch their Mandates will be no less than in the days of Moses!"

The Lord said, "What you are seeing is My plan to take over the world. My plan to raise up a remnant and My plan to feed the nations."

Stage 4 - Shaking

Stage 4 is a time of great shaking marked by massive calamity worldwide, a calamity that has not been seen before. Very little will remain. Very little will stand. Truly a time and season for the survival of the fittest. The shaking will impact systems, structures, and all people including the Saints.

There will however be a remnant of people as well as a remnant of the Systems and Structures. The Systems and Structures will not continue to function at this time due to the severity of the shaking. I, Cheryl-Ann, wondered how a system or structure could have a "remnant". It is at this point that the Lord reminded me of a well known missionary. She recently returned to a location in China from where she had to flee during her early years of her ministry. In her recent return to the area, she found a remnant of the people she had served as well as a remnant the church itself. The physical location had moved, but there remained a remnant of its existence just the same. Somehow, God is going to have His remnant of people, systems and structures.

Stage 5 – Glory People

Stage 5 was called *Glory People*. Out of the ashes I saw a true remnant emerge; humble, meek and victorious. They will be known for their *intimacy with the Lord* which had been cultivated over the years. Out of this intimacy, He shared with them His secrets and specific ways to survive the time of shaking they had just been through. Hence, He considered them His "Glory People".

They were those who lived by the promises of God, who "faith-ed" into existence whatever they needed, who ate the scroll and became whatever it said, and who loved not their lives even unto death. These were the only ones qualified to be part of the Glory Remnant because as He said to me, "Glory cannot be where *self is*". Those who were willing to lose their lives in Stage 4, found their lives in Stage 5. They will become the bright shining lights on a hill. They will be the voice that cries out in the wilderness. They will remain on this earth until the Lord returns. They will be marked by indescribable joy because they will know for whom they lived and for whom they were willing to die.

Chapter 1: Convergence

If you are like me, you have always wanted to know God's will for your life. You know – that special thing you were created to do.

Having Desire

Since I was a child, I have had this feeling that I would be used of God in some significant way, but exactly what or how I would be used has remained uncertain. On several occasions, I have wondered, "Is this just my own desire or is it truly the will of God for my life?" How about you?

Sovereign Foundation

In the spring of 1993, I had a personal encounter with God. On an un-crowded airplane, over Los Angeles, I heard an audible voice say, "Learn the Law!" Mind you, this is the only such experience like this I have ever had. And like any unique experience, I had no reference point to decide what to do about it.

At first, I felt I was mistaken and maybe overheard someone around me; but there really was nobody sitting near me. I was reading the airline's magazine, which is always in the seat back pocket, and as I turned to the next page, I was shaken. On that page was an article about how mid-level executives were going to law school and getting their Juris Doctor (JD) degree instead of getting a Masters in Business Administration (MBA). What a coincidence, I thought. I must tell you, it bothered me. As the announcement for landing broke my concentration, I tried to dismiss what had just happened as anything but a word from God.

You see, I am not a perfect person. I make mistakes all the time. As I said earlier, God doesn't speak to me - - especially in an audible way. At that time, I was, at best, a back-slidden Baptist. It was not in my doctrine to even think this could happen. I thought to myself that it must have been bad airplane food (they did feed you in those days).

Taking Action

Upon returning home to Colorado Springs from my business trip, I tried to dismiss what had happened on the airplane. First, I had no use for lawyers. It had been my business experience that if you needed a lawyer, you likely were in trouble. Second, I really did not want to go back to school; I already had a successful business. Lastly, I was not what you would call religious; what would my family and friends think? Nevertheless, every morning when I awoke, there it was again, not audible as the first time, but almost always my first thought.

So I decided to look into it. I bought a book on applying to law school. This was pre-Internet, otherwise I would have just "Googled it!" As I began to call various law schools, I found that in order for me to go to law school in the fall, I would have to take an exam called an LSAT. It was now May and the last exam was in February. The more I was told it would not happen this year, the more I persisted. For someone who did not want to go to law school, I was obsessed with getting in by the fall of 1993.

Divine Appointment

I discovered that there were three schools that might allow me to start in the fall; they were the Birmingham School of Law, Mercer School of Law in Atlanta, and the University of Arkansas at Little Rock. Of course, Birmingham is where my wife's father and family lived and "never living in Birmingham" was a vow I made but that is a whole different story! Atlanta was a big city, but I could see living there, and I knew nothing about Little Rock.

So I planned a trip to fly to Birmingham and apply there first, get turned down, flip my coin, and either go east to Atlanta or go west to Little Rock next.

With no appointment, I went to meet the Dean of the law school in Birmingham. As I sat outside Dean Locke's office, his secretary said, "You don't have an appointment; Dean Locke is very busy today." I said, "I will just wait." And so I did for eight hours as he passed in an out of his office and never once acknowledged me.

Leaving for my wife's grandmother's home that evening, I felt defeated, even foolish. After all, I had flown 1,500 miles without an appointment. Truthfully, I had not made application either! Planning to flip my coin and depart for my second "No" in the morning, I went to bed. The next morning, I decided to not give up so easily and I made plans to go to the law school for just one hour, try it again, and then leave Birmingham.

I was there early and as Dean Locke came in, he asked, "Who are you?" I said, "I have a quick story to tell you. You will think I am crazy, and then I will be on my way!" He said, "That is interesting, come in." As I began to tell my story about the airplane, he asked me more and more about my life. Our few minute meeting turned into two hours. He said, "Mr. Needham, let me see if I have this right. You flew all the way from Colorado Springs without an appointment, no LSAT, no application, and we don't even have your grades from your undergraduate work, right?" I said, "Yes, that is right."

Taking his legal pad which had been in front of him the whole time, and which he had not taken one note, he pushed it toward me and said, "Write this down... I will move my family from Colorado Springs to Birmingham and attend this law school and graduate... now sign your name." Then he said something hard to believe, "Well that's it Mr. Needham, you matriculate in the fall...now keep your promise." No LSAT, no application, no grades - - just my testimony and I was admitted to law school. (***Unmerited Favor***)

I later learned as we were walking out, this was his last act as Dean of the law school. He put on his hat and retired. His family had owned the law school for over 90 years and had sold it the day before (this is why he was so busy). Three years later, when I graduated, he returned to the law school to see if I had kept my promise.

Divine Training, Assignments, and Mentoring
Upon graduation, I got caught up in myself and wanted to make some money. It had been three long years and I was distracted by a job offer, forgetting I did this because God asked me to. I never thought to ask God what He wanted. (Are you guilty of this behavior too?)

I suspect that most Christians forget to ask God first. As a result we get in all sorts of misaligned relationships. In all honesty, I too have made this mistake too often.

This began my "wilderness experience." I would never practice law; I would have numerous business successes and failures; I tried to start my ministry several times, but I always failed. As part of my ministry journey, I attended a 52-week school of ministry only to discover I did not want to be a pastor. I just never asked God, "What do you want me to do Lord?"

Despite all the failures or setbacks, I had favor. I was made an Elder; I was elected to the state board of Elders; I taught discipleship studies; I did mission's work; I became an Administrative Elder, and much more. During this time I wrote several books and started several new companies. All of these efforts prepared me "for such a time as this;" I guess I should have just asked God; it likely would have saved me time and pain.

In fact, these distractions were such that I had almost forgotten I was called in 1993. At the end of 2008, I wrote a book called *Wealth 3.0 – Saving America One Small Business At A Time*. In 2009, the entire world was in financial crisis. By November of that year, I realized if I did not change the direction of my business, it would fail, and I would be bankrupt. As I write this book, it has now been almost 18 years since the experience on the airplane.

Over these years, I have witnessed a "pattern" of the Holy Spirit at work in my life. First, *out of crisis I get an idea* that I meditate on. Next, I *write a White Paper* (a short study or expression of that idea). Ultimately, I *write a book* about that journey. Mostly I have written books not to sell, but rather to birth a concept and make clear certain ideals so others and I could move forward. Some folks call this a catharsis.

Next, I used the book as my guide to take the next step. Along the way I shared my book with others, such as you, and that becomes my way of communicating God's plan and receiving favor. (By the way, I have over 50,000 of my books in the hands of readers.)

This time, however, seems different. I wrote the White Paper (called *Concept Management Company – CMC*) for an entirely different purpose and God created the unmerited favor before I wrote this book. I did not realize it until I spoke with my pastor that this is a sign I was in "Convergence." **Because of that wisdom, "for such a time as this," I have asked my Senior Pastor, Mark Schrade, to come alongside me and add wisdom to this work. Mark will provide the biblical background and context for the balance of this book. I have marked the sections with his contributions with this symbol:** Ⓜ.

> *"One of the things I learned about Convergence is that it is hard to see looking forward. However, if you look backward at your life, you can see God's hand at work."*

Looking Back

Six years after I received the word on the airplane, I had graduated from law school, attended a school of ministry, and was already qualified as a scientist. I felt I had "Learned The Law" (Laws of Man, God and Science). However, it would not be until a crisis occurred in my life that I would sit down, listen to the Holy Spirit and write my first Christian book, called *Learn the Law – Living An Un-Ambivalent Christian Life.* I never intended to publish it; it was for me. I just needed it to get through my own tough times.

However, God does not waste anything. Shortly after writing the book, I was asked by Chipp Edwards – a ministry friend who oversees a ministry called Turning Point – to come and speak for him on two Wednesdays so he could go on a much-needed vacation. Turning Point is an in-residence drug and alcohol recovery program. I wondered why he asked me, since my father was an alcoholic, and I never had a problem with addiction; but I accepted the assignment anyway. Looking for something to teach during those two weeks, I reached for my book *Learn the Law.* I decided I would just go out there and teach a few of these concepts that God had revealed to me.

You know, God works in mysterious ways; as I taught these concepts from my book, these men were finding that they now understood why they were making such bad decisions in their life. Chipp asked me to continue and for the next seven years I taught my book over and over again in 13 week rotations to the hundreds of men who came to Turning Point on their journey to recovery.

What I did realize after awhile, is that I did have an addiction, and it was to food. During this time, I became a Type II Diabetic and I realized that if I didn't get ahold of my eating it would kill me, no different than alcohol or drugs. Now I must confess I have lost 90 pounds and need to lose 50 more so I am a work in progress and it is not easy to recover from being a carboholic.

During this same period, I would teach *Learn the Law* several times at my church as a discipleship study and I was told it helped many people learn how to hear from God more clearly about making better decisions in their lives. It seems funny and a bit ironic that although I never officially published that book, it has helped hundreds learn to make good decisions.

In December 2009, a franchise development client of mine, shared *The Concept Management Company – CMC* White Paper with his brother-in-law. He read it and said, "This could change how ministry is funded." Please understand that this is not what this White Paper was about; it was a new way to fund the purchase of franchise concepts in these difficult times. However, David Auterson read it with a vision from the Holy Spirit as the way ministry could be funded in the 21st Century.

This led to David and I meeting and his sharing what he read in my White Paper. It put to a blaze that which had been just an ember since 1993. Since January of 2010, David and I have spent countless hours in meetings all over this country with literally thousands of pastors sharing what God revealed to both of us. I will share more on this later.

> *"What I hope you see is that as you walk out your calling, God will give you a vision, he will give you divine appointments, divine assignments, and training. He will add others in your life to guide you until your Convergence emerges and you begin to execute God's call [will] in your life."*

Seeking Wisdom and Finding Patterns of God's Hand

Seeing unmerited favor like never before in my life, I scheduled a meeting with my Senior Pastor, Mark Schrade. Over lunch, I shared the story of my life much as I have with you, what was currently going on in my life, and the evidence of this unmerited favor. He prayed over our lunch and began to draw on a note pad from a book he had read called, *Leadership Emergence Patterns,* by Dr. Robert Clinton.

Dr. Robert Clinton—Leadership Emergence Patterns

Sovereign Foundation	Early Life Development	Ministry Development	Convergence	Afterglow
God Chooses You	Divine Contacts Divine Mentors Word Items Life Maturity	Ministry Tasks Specialized Training Ministry Experience	Early Training Emergence Divine Contacts Maximize All That Has Developed Before	Mentoring Others

Mark told me, 'it was obvious that I had reached Convergence.' As I listened to him, I could see my whole life flash before my eyes. Every step, every good and bad decision, every event and meeting were ordered steps guided by the Lord. I was at peace and fearful all at the same time. It had been confirmed, but was I really ready? The answer is "yes", because I am not the author of my future – God is! Sure, I get to drive the bus, but God never gives us an assignment that He does not prepare and equip us for in advance. The challenge for God is for us to finally realize that. I guess I am a slow learner (1993 – 2011).

Ⓜ I have asked Mark to provide some more detail and insight here:

Kingdom Purpose
The story is told of famous scientist Albert Einstein who was once traveling from Princeton by train. When the conductor came down the aisle, punching the tickets of every passenger, he came to Einstein. Einstein reached in his vest pocket. He couldn't find his ticket, so he reached in his trouser pockets. It wasn't there, so he looked in his briefcase but couldn't find it. Then he looked in the seat beside him. He still couldn't find it.

The conductor said, "Dr Einstein, I know who you are. I'm sure you bought a ticket. Don't worry about it." Einstein nodded appreciatively. The conductor continued down the aisle punching tickets. As he was ready to move to the next car, he turned around and saw the great physicist down on his hands and knees looking under his seat for his ticket. The conductor rushed back and said again, "Dr Einstein, don't worry, I know who you are. You don't need to find your ticket. I am sure you bought one."

Einstein looked at him and said, "Young man, I too, know who I am. What I don't know is where I'm going." Do you know where you are going? Why are you here?

Isaiah 43:10 tells us that God formed us for His glory! Jesus said, "I have brought you glory on earth by completing the work you gave me to do (John 17:4)." God created you in his image with glory (Ps 8:5), good works to shine in this world that bring glory to God (Matt 5:16). Marcus Buckingham has said, "Every person is capable of doing something better than the next 10,000 people." But you must believe God wants to demonstrate His glory through you.

Thomas Edison said, "If we did all the things we are capable of doing, we would literally astonish ourselves." "Death isn't the greatest loss in life," according to Norman Cousins; "the greatest loss is what dies inside of us while we live." According to the Congressional Research Service, in its 2006 report, the average life expectancy in the United States is 77.5 years or 28,287 days! Scientist tell us that although human DNA is basically the same, yet there are up to 3 million differences in your unique genetic code from everyone else on the planet unless you are an identical twin. That means that you are not only different from anyone else alive today, but that you are uniquely different from anyone else who has ever lived! ***Don't you think you ought to find out what God's assignment and purpose is for your life?***

Kingdom Plans

As already noted, God's Kingdom Plan is for you to emerge into Kingdom Convergence for His glory. ***Convergence is the merging of all that God has been doing in a believer's life through sovereign foundations, early life and ministry development to enable them to reach their highest Kingdom potential.*** The Lord then takes that person and matches him with a Kingdom Assignment to produce the believer's most lasting influence.

Let's "Google" Esther

"...and who knows but that you have come to this royal position for such a time as this?" (Esther 4:14)

Esther's Convergence Model

Sovereign Foundation	Early Life Development	Ministry Development	Convergence
Jewish orphan in Shushan. Persia	Raised by her cousin Mordecai	Mordecai mentors and awakens her to Kingdom Calls	Impacts the laws of the land
	Mordecai was an official in the palace	Saves Jews	Rules in government
	Esther learned Judaism and Aristocratic culture	Learns the power of prayer	Saves Jews
		Puts her life on the line to save Jews	

Kingdom Process

The number one reason why people do not make it into divine Convergence is that they do not understand the process through which the Lord emerges each one of us in the Kingdom. Esther had "prominence without purpose." She, like many successful business men and women, had found favor and the "best place" in their business (Esther 2:9), yet had not discovered her Kingdom calling. We believe that Pareto's Principle (The 80/20 Rule) applies here and several studies indicate that only 20% of Christians have acted on their Convergence.

That means 80% never make it into the Convergence God has ordained for them before the foundation of the world (Eph 2:10).

Along the journey of God developing your competence and business skill, the Lord will be working on your Kingdom Character.

- Joseph has a phenomenal dream, only to be thrown into a pit, and ultimately, a prison.

- David is anointed king, kills the giant Goliath, but then spends the next years of his life running from Saul who is trying to murder him. He lost his job, wife, and best friend, on his way to Convergence.

- Daniel's Convergence came in the process of his Babylonian captivity. God had developed his character (Dan 1:18). Now the Lord would use his "excellent spirit" (Dan 5:12, 14; 6:3) to influence the government and culture.

One of the reasons believers don't influence business, government, education and culture more is because we don't know how to excel. When you stand up, compared to other people, you should stand out! God has called you to be a king and priest (Rev 1:6), and to reign on the Earth (Rom 5:17; Rev 5:10). Being in Convergence means that you should rise to the top of your field for Kingdom advancement and the glory of God!

Kingdom Perspective
The C.S. Lewis novel "Narnia: The Lion, Witch and the Wardrobe," has been made into a motion picture. One of the opening scenes depicts Lucy opening the door to another world of adventure that reveals God's Kingdom Plan for her life. Erwin McManus described such experiences as "defining moments."

The Greek word used in I Corinthians 15:52 for moment is "ATOMO." We get our English word for "Atom" from this root. An atom is the smallest part of an element, yet has nuclear power capabilities. Such are the moments in our lives. We must seize the moments God has placed before us so that we can reach His desired Convergence for our lives.

In the 1989 movie "Dead Poet Society," actor Robin Williams portrayed a teacher who sought to inspire his students not to settle for life as "Que Sera Sera," or, "whatever will be, will be," but to "Carpe Diem," "seize the day" and make the most of our opportunities (Eph 5:16). Choices can create defining moments and bring us into a period of strategic breakthrough and greatness for the glory of God.

Oliver Wendell Holmes once said, "Most people die with their music still in them." John Greenleaf Whittier has concluded, "Of all the sad words of tongue or pen, the saddest words are these: it might have been." Choose to develop your character and discover your Kingdom calling and gifts. Socrates said it well: "To move the world we must first move ourselves." As we learned in the movie Madagascar, "you got to move it, move it!" Ⓜ

Lesson – Learned
As we go through life with all of its dangers and opportunities (which are really the same thing depending on your viewpoint), and even though we often get distracted (exercising our free will), God has His sovereign hand on our life.

We are all called to His purpose; but looking forward we cannot see it. We are often just too caught up in the moment. However, what I have learned is that if we will just stop for a moment and turn around, looking back through our lives, we can see God's plan operating in our lives.

We have charted for you the steps from 1993 to 2011 of my (Robert's) Convergence in hopes it will help you do the same. As you read this book we hope it will inspire you to see God's will in your life. This book is about a big change that is needed in the world. Why me? Why now? Simply, this is all I know; it is my Convergence and if it is God's will, then nothing more matters. It is not about you or I; it is about discovering God's sovereign will for your life and having the faith right now to act on that alone.

- 1993 "Learn The Law" word received

- 1996 Ministry attempted and failed

- 1999 Prophetic Dream and Learn The Law book written

- 2000 I began to teach at Turning Point

- 2006 Franchise Book and numerous White Papers written

- 2008 Wealth 3.0 book completed as the economy crashes

- 2009 More White Papers and Conferences

- 2010 My Convergence Began

- 2011 I wrote this book

Bottom line:

> *God has His call on every person. Regardless of your skills, failures, shortcomings or accomplishments God can and will use you. Life is messy, but God will prepare you for your Convergence. The question is, will you recognize and act on it?*

Assignment #1.

Take out a few sheets of paper and ask God to reveal His plan to you. Now look back and determine when God first established His **sovereign foundation** in your life and when He began to establish **divine appointments, mentors, and assignments** preparing you for your call. More importantly, when it happened, did you, by your own free will, choose to go another direction? Once you get clarity on this, I am certain God will move you closer to your Convergence and give you the unmerited favor to accomplish His will for you. We have provided you the chart that follows to help you model where you are in your Convergence journey.

Your Convergence Model — Fill In The Blanks

Sovereign Foundation	Early Life Development	Ministry Development	Convergence

Notes:

Chapter 2: Crisis, Chaos, Change

As you read this book, you will discover that there are themes in your life that continue to repeat themselves (patterns) which become more refined over time. I suppose it is a lesson we are to learn or share or birth as a part of our calling. Some call it being continually laid at the foot of the cross. (What is your perspective?)

For me, understanding crisis, fear, and learning how to make wise decisions in the midst of confusion has been one of those repetitive patterns.

Understanding Crisis

My education into crisis began with a book I wrote in 1990 called, *Is There Life After Debt?* A business associate and I were in crisis; this crisis sprang forth from our making poor investment decisions about the use of credit in our attempt to earn wealth (using debt as a lever – see Chapter 5). My mother often said to me, "Son, you can't borrow your way to wealth (using debt)." I am continually amazed that the older I get, the smarter my parents become! We could all agree that what is true for us, should be true for our nation.

[1]For the purposes of this book, we used Dictionary.com to find the definition of Crisis and other key words throughout this book. We then merged these multiple definitions into one or more sentences which illustrate our point.

> **Crisis**[1] – A stage or sequence of events which constitute a turning point (between danger and opportunity) in social,

economic, political, or international affairs leading to a decisive change.

Wow. Is it any wonder that our leadership in Washington says, "Never miss a good opportunity to get it through in a Crisis!" In fact, one might speculate that "crisis events" have been so "staged or sequenced" to lead the country toward a "decisive change." (After all, in the last election, we all wanted change, didn't we?)

Assignment #2

So what recent events in your life at home, work, or in the government have you experienced crisis? How did you respond? Did you see danger or opportunity? What real change did you have to make? Take some time to write this out and understand how you respond to Crisis.

I know as a small business owner, when the economy in late 2008 crashed and credit dried up, finding capital to grow my business was impossible. I know many businesses that have failed since. They failed not because they were bad companies, but their business plan and cash flow were financed with credit. Until they could collect on their receivables (using debt as a lever) and pay their bills, there simply were not enough funds to cover the cost of operations. When the market crashed, receivables delayed even more, sales canceled, and the cash to meet obligations (to bridge) was impossible to borrow. Big and small businesses alike failed (i.e. Lehman Brothers). When this happens a business must dramatically cut expenses, increase income, and/or simply go out of business.

Cooking Frogs

In several of my books, I always tell the story of how you cook a frog. You place the frog in cool water and he settles down, then you slowly turn the heat up and as he enjoys the cozy warm bath. As the heat gets higher and higher, he soon cooks in his own juices. This is what happened to all of us. We believed the World Economic System (Mammon's) lie. We went against our own best good sense. We bought houses we could not afford and we enjoyed the good life on credit cards we could not pay. Of course in both cases we were bombarded by the "standards of our culture through media advertising to pursue instant gratification in lieu of good sense. The house became an "investment." The credit card was used to "save money" for an item on sale. In short we mortgaged our future for the pleasures of today. In *Is There Life After Debt?*, I called this the Wimpey Syndrome, "I will gladly pay you Tuesday for a hamburger today!" These were the famous words of Popeye's friend Wimpey.

Take a look at the financial industry, specifically mortgages. Wall Street took advantage of changes in certain laws (Glass-Stegall Act 1932, Bank Holding Company Act 1956, and Gramm–Leach–Bliley Act 1999) that allowed hedge funds to basically take bets on the American Dream and securitize mortgage notes and other notes while enabling banks to own brokerage and insurance under one umbrella. By 2008 this behavior had reached crisis which led to more government control of the market and financial institutions (The Dodd–Frank Wall Street Reform and Consumer Protection Act 2010).

A good friend of mine, Neil Garfield, JD, writes a blog called LivingLies (livinglies.wordpress.com) where he has written thousand of pages on this crisis in America. Neil says this "sequence of events" looked something like this:

- Wall Street Banks created a bond that derived its value from mortgage loans. The bond was to be paid from a pool of assets. The Banks reduced the pool of money by reducing the funding of mortgages far less than the investors knew. By doing this they had guaranteed from the start that the pool would never be able to pay off the Bond.

- As a cover for their misbehavior, the banks diverted attention to the mortgage lending process that was also geared to make loans that were guaranteed to fail so they could point the finger at mortgage defaults instead of their own treachery.

- Wall Street creates a product called Credit Default Swaps, which are bets that the pool would fail to make payments on the Bond.

- Wall Street sells this product extremely well. In fact, they do it so well that they are flushed with more money than they can use for mortgages even under their existing plan. So the banks go to the market for more mortgages; however, the criteria for qualifying for a mortgage is too difficult for the average consumer, so Wall Street gets the government to lower the criteria for qualifying for a mortgage, and they create "option loans" where a person can pay less than even the accruing interest, which raises the amount due.

- More mortgages are treated as securitized, but the paperwork to transfer the loans to the pools is intentionally left out so the banks can assert themselves as "pretender lenders" in order to sell the same loans multiple times.

- The Banks are still selling too well and they have exhausted all the people that could be new borrowers, so they expand the loans by inflating the value in the homes, so real estate agents get the sellers to raise the price, mortgage brokers get appraisers to increase appraisals, buyers are shopping for lower monthly payments, so "teaser" payments are lowered to get the borrower to sign and the government lowers the interest rate.

- The demand has risen even more as worldwide investors want in. The demand for more mortgage loans increases, speculators enter the market with strategies to buy more than one house or condo, hoping to flip them for a quick profit and never expecting it to end. Stated income applications make the way for anyone who can fog a mirror to qualify (FICO Scores of 450 and up). The system (scheme) makes more and more money for the banks and Wall Street.

- Fund managers unaware of the actual events in the marketplace and comforted by assurances of insurance and Triple-A ratings from bond rating agencies, use our retirement funds to buy these supposedly safe instruments, trying to improve the return on investment.

- **Then sudden destruction.** When the demand exceeded the supply, banks began selling the mortgages to Wall Street more than once into these securitization pools, thereby defrauding the investors, insurance companies, and even homeowners. The house of cards came crashing down. This last step is criminal, but no one has gone to jail yet. Cover up?

The results of this crisis have all but destroyed the economics of our country and most of the world. Why did this happen? Over 100 Million transactions were treated as securitized and the outcome is far from clear as to whether the mortgages or the 10 million foreclosures, so far, will stand or be reversed. At least 10 million more now face foreclosure. In some markets, housing prices have returned to reality, which unfortunately is below 50% of the original asking price. What are we to do?

Remember a crisis is a sequence of events which leads to a decisive change. For those of us who believe as Christians, we should have seen this coming. We have trusted the World System too long and now we have been sucked into this financial disaster. It is our own fault; the Bible foretold of these events, but we believed the world more. Is this the beginning of the promised plan to change to a global economy? Before we answer this question, let's contrast crisis and chaos.

Chaos versus Crisis.
Since we have already taken a close look at Crisis, let's compare its definition to the definition[1] of Chaos.

Chaos – a state of total confusion with a lack of organization or order.

Wow again. It would seem this is how we all got confused, but clearly this was no accident; it was planned and it had an order to it – decisive change! So quickly we can dismiss Chaos as a theory, but we all knew that, because they told us in advance it would be a "world changing crisis." This is like "hiding in plain sight."

What we must all do is choose how we decide to respond. We can either continue to follow the plan to certain destruction or we can create change ourselves to a system that was developed for us a long time ago. We will explore this plan in greater detail later in this book. For now let's focus on the concept of Change by Fear first, then Wisdom.

Change by Fear.
The global leaders need us scared, to get quick change in before we all wake up. Think about all those bills that passed without our Congress ever reading any of them, based solely on fear. Now Congress just passed a bill that will allow the President to declare anyone who "radically opposes" his plan to be declared a terrorist! What happened to our Constitution? Truthfully, this book could be deemed radical thinking.

In defining Change, consider this definition[1]:

> **Change:** To make the form or substance of the future of something different (transformed, converted, altered or modified) from what it would be if just left alone.

Ⓜ   Pastor Mark, help our readers to understand this change by fear from a biblical perspective.

The Perfect Economic Storm
The Perfect Storm was a 2000 dramatic disaster film starring George Clooney that described a fishing boat crew, desperate for money, which got caught in the "perfect storm" of 1991, and never made it out alive. In October of 1991, a dying tropical hurricane from Bermuda collided with

a cold front from the Great Lakes, resulting in the incredible impact of 100 foot waves and financial and personal destruction.

Robert has already described when the dying hurricane of "supply" met the "cold front" of demand, the "perfect economic storm" was created. Recent plunging home values, declining stocks, fluctuating oil and gas prices, vanishing credit, soaring food prices, budget deficits and the falling value of the dollar are all evidences of the devastating results of our recent economic storm. No wonder it has been characterized by "bailouts" in the U.S. and abroad. A suggested cover story for the American consumer might be, "Best Investment Now: Antacids!"

Fears:

"Honey, I've Shrunk the Portfolio!"
As a result of the "Perfect Storm," many have responded in fear. According to a poll conducted by Decipher, Inc. and Yahoo Finance in July 2008, American's top 5 personal financial fears were...

1. Rising cost of living

2. Economic downturn and job insecurity

3. Consumer debt

4. The housing crisis

5. Lack of savings

Fear is the most negative emotion known to man. Fear is defined as a sense of dread, panic, apprehension or terror. It can range from a fear of real physical danger to pathological phobias. Researchers tell us that we are born with only two fears: the fear of falling and the fear of loud noises. All other fears are "learned responses." If all other fears are learned responses, what is our culture teaching us?

USC sociologist Barry Glassner has described our country as a "culture of fear." Crime is featured on our newspaper stands, radio and television stations and websites. Misleading statistics create a sense of panic among consumers. After the Great Depression, Franklin Delano Roosevelt sought to restore consumer confidence in his presidential inaugural address when he said, "There is nothing to fear but fear itself." But because 80% of our decisions are based upon our emotions, fear can have devastating effects upon us. A gloom and doom forecast may lead to some reasonable predictions, **but fear shouldn't be the foundation of our decisions.** Ron Blue states that **fear-based decisions** may be characterized by one or more of the following traits:

- The decision is made quickly, with little forethought.

- The decision is presumptive, based on conclusions that have little or no substantiating proof.

- The decision is ill-advised, having been made under the counsel of untested, unreliable or biased sources.

A fear-based decision is often accompanied by gut reaction of anxiety and tension. By contrast, wise and thoughtful decisions are accompanied by a sense of peace and calm stability (Phil 4:7). Fear can ruin the best-laid financial plans. Remember, Christ rebuked the servant who didn't invest his talent because of fear (Matt 25:25). Too many believers today are responding to our current economic troubles like the world. "Thermometers" respond to rising uncertainty in the economy with rising emotional mercury of fear, totally forgetting how our Faith is to rule our fears in our pursuit of Kingdom Economics. Don't forget, the children of Israel missed their promised land flowing with "milk and honey" because of fear (Deut 1:25-28). "Thermostats," on the on the hand, control their temperature. They keep focused on their financial goals and control their emotions with faith in God's Word.

Rock Solid in Financial Storms
On September 19, 2008, Jason Hanna reported for CNN's iReport site about one house that was still standing when 200 homes and buildings around it were leveled to the ground by 110 mph Hurricane Ike winds. Reporters quickly located the home owners, Warren and Pam Adams. Three years earlier, the Adams' home had been destroyed by Hurricane Rita. Because they loved their beach home they hired an engineering firm to raise their new residence above the other homes on wooden columns. The foundation was made with reinforced concrete and the builders followed the latest hurricane building codes to the letter. The moral to this story is this: "storms will inevitably come, but blessed is the person who has built their economics and faith on the word of God (Matt 7:24-27)."

You're Invited to the "Tea Party!"
The world is "crying-out" for change! The "Tea Party" Movement is a conservative and libertarian grass roots uprising to produce change. Supporters endorse reduced government spending, oppose raising taxes, and desire to reduce our national debt, balance the federal budget and interpret the constitution from its original intent. But what produced this protest? Simply, our latest financial crisis and our overwhelming fears of more financial abuse to come.

Occupy Wall Street began with a Canadian activist group called "Adbusters" on September 17th, 2011 in Zucotti Park near the Wall Street financial district in NYC. They also want change! They are protesting against social and economic inequality, high unemployment, corporate corruption and corporation's undue influence on government. The "99%" want to change the balance of economic wealth in this country and around the world! By the way a similar group in London have just been declared Terrorist... is this an indicator of the future response here? Stand on faith!

Turning Points: A Pathway for Change
We live in a world where "business as usual" is "change!" New initiatives, technology and staying ahead of the competition are driving the way we work. "Change is the only constant," according to ancient Greek philosopher, Heraclitus. But what is producing the changes in your business and finances?

A "turning point" is a planned or unplanned event that changes the previous course of a thing. Robert has already described how that a crisis can constitute a turning point and lead to changes whether temporary or permanent. A crisis can clarify your focus, change your priorities and test your faith. However, many times change brought about by a crisis is short-lived. Have you ever known people who are continually in a crisis? They never learn or acquire the wisdom from their last crisis to keep them out of the next one.

Fear can also bring about a turning point that leads to a temporary or permanent change, although almost always a negative one. Unreal fears paralyze us with a million "what if's." Many are bound up with the fear of making the wrong decision, the fear of failure, the fear that nothing will change. But the only thing fear should do for the believer is to motivate us to call on God who has not given us a spirit of fear, but of "power, love and a delivered [sound] mind" (2 Tim 1:7).

Are You Smarter than a 5th Grader?
"Are You Smarter than a 5th Grader?" Is an American game show played by a single contestant who attempts to answer ten questions (plus a bonus question) taken from elementary school text books. Each "correct answer" increases the "amount of money the player banks," reaching a maximum of $100,000. Along the way, the player can be assisted by one of five school age kids. Notably, upon getting an answer incorrect the contestant must state that they are not "smarter than a 5th grader!" I believe we are losing the Kingdom Wealth available to us today because we don't have the elementary answers of financial wisdom from God's Word!

The Book of Proverbs was not written like many books in the Bible, to a group of people collectively. But this book of wisdom was written to the individual, from Solomon to his son, from God the Father to His children. It was written to help one develop a "better life." You will find the word "better" used fifteen times in Proverbs contrasting the better life wisdom brings in comparison to being foolish. Proverbs screams at believers eighty times to not be "foolish." To be foolish is to be mentally naïve, thick-headed, worldly and spiritual irresponsible. However, "Wisdom is better than rubies and nothing we desire can be compared to her" (Prov 8:10b). Wisdom calls to all (1:20-23), but laughs at those who spurred wisdom when they fall into a crisis (1:26).

Get Smart
Get Smart was a 2008, American spy-fi comedy that revolved around our American Intelligence Agency, "Control," combating the terrorist organization "Kaos." It's time that we, as believers come out of the "Chaos" in the world's economy and "get control" of God's Kingdom Economics for this hour.

> *The Lord founded the earth by wisdom. By His understanding He established the heavens. By His knowledge, the seas were divided and dew came from heaven.* Proverbs 3:19-20

These verses of Scripture describe the dynamic part that knowledge, understanding and wisdom played in the creation of the Universe. Through wisdom God transformed "Chaos into Order!" Likewise, if God can bring permanent order out of continuous chaos in the natural order, what can he do with his people in the spiritual and natural realms if we get into divine order with His Kingdom Economics today?

Ⓜ Thanks Mark. Lastly, let's look at how to make how to make wise decisions in the midst of confusion.

Wise Decisions

A cornerstone of Wisdom lies in the meaning of the Chinese characters for "CRISIS". It is represented by two symbols:

The Chinese Symbol for Crisis

For years, I, like so many other authors, interpreted the Chinese word for Crisis "wēijī [危机]" as the intersection of Danger and Opportunity. While loosely translated this is somewhat correct, but more accurately translated, it means the intersection of "danger – wēi" and "the critical moment when change occurs – jī". Considering that Opportunity can occur when we change, it could be correct; however, if our change is even further wrong, then it could lead to even more Crisis in our life. The point is, when your life seems to be in Crisis, the natural instinct is to fear the Danger. A better response would be: "Is it now time to find the Opportunity?" See the Danger as the Distraction, and the Opportunity as the hope.

Truthfully, I believe at the center of this fork in the road is a tree and too often we decide to exercise our free will and choose neither danger nor opportunity, but INDECISION. In Revelation 3:15 – 16 KJV, speaking to the Church at Laodicea, Jesus stated, "I know thy works, that thou art neither cold nor hot: I would thou wert cold or hot. So then because thou art lukewarm, and neither cold nor hot, I will spew thee out of my mouth." See, Jesus can work with you Hot or Cold, just not lukewarm. If you choose indecision, you become a "tree victim" and will be constantly laid at the foot of the cross. For you see, the tree at the intersection is the cross of Christ. If you choose wrongly, God will give you another opportunity to correct that decision. Therefore, there is no bad decision, except to not make a decision at all.

Take Pastor Mark's suggestion, and read Proverbs; there are 31 chapters. Might I suggest that you take three months reading a chapter a day so that you have read it three times. This surely will help you obtain the wisdom to make decisions. Find some other people who are following the same path and do this exercise together so you get the most out of it.

Chapter 3: Wealth and Freedom

Lutcher, mullah, cheddar, greenbacks, dollars, cash .... No matter what you call it, the means of exchange to purchase goods and services is called Currency.

Currency is defined[1] as the money in use in a country. Money is defined[1] as pieces of metal or certificates (paper) used to buy and sell.

Therefore, for our discussion let's expand Currency to mean the way commerce takes place within a country bearing an image of a person or thing that that country holds in high regard either made of metal or paper that enables its citizens to have the faith to buy or sell goods and services.

In Chapter 2, we introduced you to the term Mammon. We know what God is, but who or what is Mammon? There are two perspectives on this word Mammon. First, it simply is synonymous for money (Currency). Second, and maybe more controversial, is that Mammon[2] is a demonic "power" in heavenly places (Circa: Middle Ages) which controls world finances and when we choose the benefits of money over God's resources, we are worshiping Mammon. If you look at various translations in the Greek, Hebrew, Aramaic, and Latin, Mammon is wealth, riches, money or a loan. The Chaldeans translated it "confidence". In pop culture, Mammon is referred to often as a demon in software, games, books, videos and movies. Since the Bible chose to capitalize its reference to Mammon, we accepted the demon status. If correct, then when we attempt to manage our finances, we are in spiritual warfare between heaven and hell or more particularly between World Economics (Satan) and Kingdom Economics (God).

Further, we are told that true wealth comes from only God. So what do we call the accumulation of Currency in the Earth? It is called Assets. Assets are defined[1] as items of ownership convertible into cash (Currency or money); the total resources of a person or business, as cash, notes receivable and accounts receivable, securities, inventories, goodwill, skills, organizational value, fixtures, machinery, precious metals, or real estate. Since all these are derived from Currency (cash) first, for our purposes they are all referred to as Assets.

Assets are defined as the accumulation of Currency above the basic needs; if you will the money you can save beyond basic needs or can be used for an emergency.

By comparison, that which occurs naturally or is given by God is true Wealth. **We will not use man's definition of Wealth in this book as it for all purposes is the same as our definition for Assets.**

In Chapter 6 we will expand our thinking on Wealth as it is defined in the Kingdom Economy, but for now, let's talk of Wealth in more general terms.

Sub-Creators

God's Wealth is infinite since He is the Creator. This is hard to accept at first, because we think of the Earth as finite and the Universe is infinite; but God owns the Universe and the Earth is part of the Universe. Further, since He has made us Sub-Creators (Gen 2:20, Gen 9:7), therefore His Wealth is being multiplied in the Earth all the time. One way of understanding our role as Sub-Creators is by affirming that God is the owner of all Creation. We are subcontractors of His Creation (assigned by the general Creator) and given the raw materials to use for our Wealth creation; as derived from nature, life, culture, society, intellect and family. We are charged with mixing these raw materials with our God-given talents. We have been commanded to increase or multiply the world, to build it up, to transform it and to "subdue" it (Gen 1:28). We can mix the original Creation into new things that did not exist at the time of Creation, but we never have title (ownership) over our own creations as they are subordinated to God's Creation; however, we are free to use them for our own and the world's benefit.

Despite our investment of labor and talent, (even as improved or multiplied by our mixture), the original title to all things still belongs to God, for He is sovereign. However, we are given the right to increase this **Wealth through multiplication for our own needs and purposes as Sub-Creators for God.**

> **Consider wheat**. From a single grain ultimately an entire field of wheat can be created. It takes time, but God's ability to multiply man's combination of time and talent in the Earth, has given man the ability to *"sow single seed – feed a nation."* All of this can be done without Mammon's Currency.
>
> **Now consider Jesus**; from His single perfect seed, God created the salvation for the entire world.

This understanding of the power of Seed Faith is critical to what we hope you will learn from this book. In fact, if you learn this principle, frankly, you won't need much else. **God's Kingdom Economic System is based on our use of Seed Faith and Multiplication.** We will explore this even more in Chapter 6.

So what is the difference between the two different economic systems? We believe the chart that follows will help you see the picture more clearly.

Mammon: The World Economic System	God: The Kingdom Economic System
It is about Buying and Selling.	It is about Giving and Receiving.
Currency earned by people from their labor (Cain) and Interest earned on Assets invested. **Usually leads to trusting things more than God.** (Idolatry)	Wealth that naturally occurs in the Earth which can multiplied by our time and talent then converted to Assets or Currency to fulfill God's covenants, purpose and calling with men.
If Currency is your desire and God is your means to it, then you are using God as a vending machine.	If God is your desire and Currency is a means to serve Him, this is the right Order in the Kingdom of God.
Faith in Currency leads to destruction and eternal death.	Faith in God leads to salvation and eternal life.

Percentage Increase vs. Multiplication

Percentage Increase is a World Economic System concept of Asset (wealth) building. When we earn Currency from our labor that is greater than our Maslow Needs (see Chapter 6) it is called discretionary income. We cannot invest our Currency for the future until our basic needs are met. If you recall, my mother once said, "you cannot borrow your way to success or happiness." (See Chapter 5 – Debt As A Lever).

Much like our How You Cook A Frog analogy in Chapter 2, the World Economic System used banking to convince us that Percentage Increase is how we can accumulate wealth (Assets).

Banking Example

$1,000 placed in a Certificate of Deposit (CD) at 4% interest earns $40, making your balance $1040 in one year. Said another way, your Percentage Increase is CD (your principal) times ($\times$) 1.04.

Rule of 72. The banking Rule of 72 is how banks and you can estimate how long it will take for your Assets to double. Here is how it works: Take 72 and "divide" it by the interest rate (Percentage Increase)

72/4% = 18 Years

In 2011, the banks are paying from 1 to 4% Percentage Increase (interest), but are charging most consumers 18 to 29% Percentage Increase on their credit cards and consumer loans. We have already determined that at 4% it takes 18 years for your funds to double and if the average person works 40 years (age 25 – 65), then 40/18 = 2.22 doubles can occur in a working lifetime. Let's round up for the benefit of a doubt to 3 doubles to be fair. That said, while your money sits at the bank for 40 years, the bank "loans" your money to other customers on credit cards, consumer loans, mortgage loans, and auto loans at rates of 18% or more. 72/18 = 4 years for bank to double your money. 40/4 = 10 possible doubles in a working lifetime.

Let's see how that works out:

For You	$1,000 Saved	For the Bank	
1. $2,000		1. $2,000	6. $64,000
2. $4,000		2. $4,000	7. $128,000
3. **$8,000**		3. $8,000	8. $256,000
		4. $16,000	9. $512,000
		5. $32,000	10. **$1,024,000**

The banks give you $8,000 back in 40 years; but on **your money** the banks have earned $1,016,000. In Chapter 5, as we look at the Federal Reserve's *Modern Money Mechanics*, we will find that it is much more than the $1Million they get to keep; it can be as much as nine times that number! Funny, the bank, which is the instrument of money management in the World Economic System, has learned to create wealth from our Assets. Now you understand why they have marble floors and we all have linoleum.

The banking system enjoys a counterfeit form of multiplication based on debt. This abomination leads to destruction of families and all we are left with is Percentage Increase to keep us happy. As we explore this further, you will 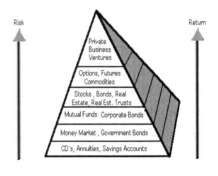 see this for what it really is, a form of economic slavery.

Call it savings accounts, investment accounts, real estate, or insurance, all of these systems are limited by the concept of Percentage Increase. **The higher the Percentage Increase, the higher the risk of loss to your principal.**

When you can finally overcome your basic needs for income, this currency becomes Assets that you can invest to earn this Percentage Increase. When your Assets earn income (your money earns money), this is considered wealth creation in the World Economic System.

Multiplication

The Kingdom Economic System offers more than a Percentage Increase on income and it is independent of your personal needs. It is provided by God from His love for you, and not because you need it, or because you have achieved a certain level of income and can now save. Consider Matthew 6: 24 – 33.

> **24** "No one can serve two masters. Either he will hate the one and love the other, or he will be devoted to the one and despise the other. You cannot serve both God and Mammon. **25** "Therefore I tell you, do not worry about your life, what you will eat or drink; or about your body, what you will wear. Is not life more important than food, and the body more important than clothes? **26** Look at the birds of the air; they do not sow or reap or store away in barns, and yet your heavenly Father feeds them. Are you not much more valuable than they? **27** Who of you by worrying can add a single hour to his life ? **28** "And why do you worry about clothes? See how the lilies of the field grow. They do not labor or spin. **29** Yet I tell you that not even Solomon in all his splendor was dressed like one of these. **30** If that is how God clothes the grass of the field, which is here today and tomorrow is thrown into the fire, will he not much more clothe you, O you of little faith? **31** So do not worry, saying, 'What shall we eat?' or 'What shall we drink?' or 'What shall we wear?' **32** For the pagans run after all these things, and your heavenly Father knows that you need them. **33** But seek first his kingdom and his righteousness, and all these things will be given to you as well. (NIV)

Earlier we discussed how **with a single seed you can feed a nation**. Think about it; everything you need to feed an entire nation is already in the Earth **and it is free without cost**. Is it because we have become lazy that we don't possess God's Wealth as He intended? Adam did not have a banker, nor did he borrow money, nor did he rely on someone to feed him, or a government to watch over him either. He subdued the Garden of Eden and did what his Father in Heaven told him to do. In the chapters that follow, we will see how we can restore our lives to these economic realities.

Understanding Freedom
Like it or not, **we must consider the belief system of those we choose to follow and entrust our lives to**. Such was the case when America was formed by our founding fathers. They drew their beliefs from a Christian well of morals and ethics to establish our Constitution and Bill of Rights. When we depart from that belief system, it leads to a failure of that dream.

Andrew Jackson and Abraham Lincoln both understood that a central banking system that created slavery of a nation's workers through a system of lending (debt), was inconsistent with the freedom our founders sought. In theory, some would say, **it was a plan of certain world power groups, since they could not control our hearts (a desire for freedom), they would enslave us through our commerce**. We just say it has been Satan's plan since he fell from Heaven.

> Let's define[1] **Freedom** as exemption from external <u>control</u>, interference, regulation, etc. The power to determine action without restraint. Political or national independence. Personal liberty, as opposed to bondage or slavery.

In America today, how has this worked out? We definitely are not exempt from external control and regulation. While we agree that the banking system, absent of regulation, created a mess that will take years to clean up, if ever, we still as believers don't want governmental control that stifles our liberty conceived by our founders which sprang forth from our Creator. In the next chapter we compare central power and how it corrupts even the very "Republic" for which our nation stands.

Further, we are constrained from determining our own action by our employers. Our employers tell us where we can live, what kind of car we can drive, and what school our children can attend by the Currency they exchange for our time and talent. If we try and escape that tyranny, we often have to borrow money which then further enslaves us to the World Economic System.

America is no longer nationally independent. We hear in the news daily that we are a part of a global economy intertwined with Europe and the rest of the world. Any one nation failing would likely start a domino effect where several nations would fail, and possibly the entire World Economic System. Now that causes fear!

Clearly we have been enslaved by Mammon's plan to use debt instruments. We are so constrained by this plan that we believe we cannot "GIVE" into the work of the ministry without risking our own financial security (and thus the Great Commission is delayed).

"GIVING" is our weapon of warfare again Satan's plan. Giving is our greatest expression of freedom in that we say to the World Economic System, "I am not bound by your belief system and status criteria, I am held in the hands of a loving God which will provide all my needs according to His riches in Glory. **He has provided me an abundance of Wealth that I can multiply to meet my needs and the needs of others who are not able to provide for themselves."**

It is our decision if we are to act on this calling. We are asking each one who reads this book to consider your role in this reformation, not against a government, not against mankind, but against Satan's plan for the destruction of God's children through the bondage of the World Economic System.

Giving and Receiving vs. Sowing and Reaping
Referring back to the Scripture cited earlier from Matthew 6:24 – 29, Jesus teaches us a very important lesson as we prepare to study how

to overcome. The World Economic System operates on buying and selling, *quid pro quo*, an exchange of this to get that.

Sowing and Reaping, while a valid spiritual law, is not how we obtain Grace and God's blessings in the Kingdom. This has often been incorrectly taught as a key part of a prosperity message. Sowing and Reaping is more akin to Buying and Selling than it is Giving and Receiving. Yet church leaders teach us to sow a seed and God will return a blessing of 30, 60, or even 100 times. In verses 26 – 28 Jesus teaches that God provides Grace such that the sparrow and the lilies need do nothing. Simply this provision has nothing to do with works. He is Jehovah Jireh – Our Provider.

That said, God does give us the power to **Sow A Seed and Feed A Nation through His Multiplying Command to us**. We however, are not sowing our seeds but His through our time and talent. Everything you need to bless yourself and the children of God is already present in the Earth. This will be expanded further.

(M)Mark, please share with us a few of your thoughts about this.

Mammon:
The Ultimate "Ponzi Scheme"
Bernard Madoff will go down in history as one of Wall Street's most notorious criminals. He cheated investors out of $65 billion and far eclipsed the 1980's insider trading scandals of junk-bond financiers Michael Milken and Ivan Boesky. Among the thousands of Madoff's victims were Hollywood celebrities such as Kevin Bacon, Larry King, Jane Fonda, Steven Spielberg and Madoff's own sister who he scammed out of $3 million. He was arrested and pleaded guilty to eleven federal offenses and in June, 2009, was sentenced to 150 years in prison.

The term "Ponzi Scheme" is the description of any scam that pays early investors with ill-gathered funds from later investors. Eight decades before Bernie Madoff's crimes, Charles Ponzi (1882-1949), held the record as the greatest swindler in American history. At the start of the

Roaring Twenties, he promised his clients a 50% profit within 45 days or 100% profit within ninety days. In the end, Ponzi was charged with more than eighty counts of mail fraud, spent years in jail and died in a charity hospital.

As Robert has pointed out in this chapter, many (even believers) are duped by the spirit of Mammon which tries to take the place of God in our lives. Pastor Jimmy Evans said, "Mammon promises us the things only God can give – security, significance, identity, independence, power and freedom."

God says, "Sow and Reap." Mammon says, "Cheat and Steal." God says, "Give and Receive." Mammon says, "Buy and Sell."

Years ago, John Milton wrote *Paradise Lost*. In this epic poem, Milton pictured Mammon as a demonic general standing beside Satan himself. Don't be deceived by Satan's Ponzi scheme that promises you ill-gathered asset gains that are not "true riches." Matthew 6:24 indicates that Mammon is also a jealous god, in that a believer cannot serve both God and Mammon. Don't serve Mammon, "For the love of money (Mammon), is the root of all evil" (I Tim 6:10).

Money, Money, Money...Money!
The Apprentice is an American reality television show hosted by businessman and television personality Donald Trump. The "Ultimate Job Interview" features sixteen to eighteen people who compete in a cut-throat elimination contest for a one-year, $250,000 starting job contract. The theme song describes this capitalistic, greed-filled show the best. "For the Love of Money", by The Ojays, symbolizes the "American Dream" in pop culture, but not the true riches God desires to bring.

True Riches?
Robert has already established that fiat currency is only the illusion of true Wealth. He stated that money is defined as pieces of metal or certificates of paper (promissory notes) used to buy and sell.

Debasement is the practice of lowering the value of currency. A coin is debased if the quantity of gold, silver, copper or nickel is reduced. Paper currency is debased when the volume of money printed exceeds the demand and is greater that the commodities which back it up. The Roman *denarius* gradually decreased in value over time as the Roman government altered both the size and the silver content of the coin to a mere 2% silver.

A post WWII Bretton Woods Agreement was developed at the United Nations Monetary and Financial Conference held in Bretton Woods, New Hampshire from July 1-22, 1944. Seven hundred and thirty delegates from forty-four allied nations developed a landmark system for a monetary exchange of currencies based upon gold. But President Richard Nixon suspended the dollar's convertibility to gold on August 15th, 1971. Since that time, the dollar has lost over 90% of its gold value according to Sue Gardner. U S coinage was also debased in the 1960's. In 1964, our silver coins contained 90% silver; in 1964, they contained just 40% silver: in 1969, they contained 0% silver according to Tom Barrett. So, what are we laboring for? Our currency is not real Wealth. God owns all the real material Wealth. The Psalmist said, "The Earth is the Lord's and the fullness thereof" (Ps 24:1). It is estimated that there are over 9 million metric tons of gold under the Earth's oceans alone!

Deal, or No Deal?
In the process of channel surfing you probably have come across the TV game show, "Deal or No Deal". The game revolves around opening a set of briefcases, each containing a different prize. Throughout the process the banker tries to offer "a deal" to the contestant to settle for a lesser amount of money. Tell the devil "No Deal" when he tries to put you in bondage to debt and selfish greed!

The Bible uses the words rich, riches and richly 180 times in Scripture. Isaiah asks, "Why spend money on what is not bread and labor for what does not satisfy?" (Isa 55:2)

Jesus spoke to the church at Laodicea and said, "You say you are rich and do not need anything: but you do not realize that you are wretched, pitiful, poor, blind and naked. I counsel you to buy from me gold refined in the fire, so you can become rich…" (Rev 3:17-18).

Assets refer to what you have, but Wealth refers to who you are. "The blessing of the Lord makes rich and adds no sorrow to it" (Prov. 10:22).

Kingdom Wealth is being rich in faith (James 2:5), good works (I Tim 6:9), as well as giving us all things to enjoy (I Tim 6:17). So, don't settle for the banker's deal to settle for mere Assets; invest in Kingdom Economics and enjoy the real Wealth God has planned.

Satan tried to make Jesus a deal when he offered Him the kingdoms of the world if He would bow down to worship him (Matt 4;9). Many who took Satan's deal found themselves robbed of true Wealth. Multimillionaire George Vanderbilt killed himself by jumping from a hotel window. U S Senator Lester Hunt, actress Marilyn Monroe and poet Ernest Hemmingway all achieved world fame and riches, but not Kingdom Wealth.

Twenty-eight countries have a national lottery. One-half of American adults spend collectively $45 billion annually on lottery games in forty states. Yet, the odds of a person winning a large "Powerball" are 1 in 120,526,770. The odds of a person winning a "Mega Million" jackpot are 1 in 135,000,000. The odds of a person winning the "Lotto" are 1 in 2 ½ billion! In fact, you have a better chance of being "struck by lightning twice a year" than you do winning the Publishers Clearing House Sweepstakes. **As believers, we don't live by luck; we live by covenant and stewardship of real Wealth.**

The Genesis Commission
Robert reminded us that God's Wealth was infinite as Creator and that we are His "Sub-Creators." In Genesis 1:28, God commissioned Adam and

Eve to be "fruitful." God placed them in a place with all the resources they needed to build a great life, but told them to sub-create with it. Even though the Lord deserves the glory for all of our accomplishments, He hasn't built one building, ship, automobile, school, or even church on the Earth.

The Genesis Commission is for people everywhere to invest, build and develop the land God gives them. John records Jesus declaring that, "This is to My Father's glory that you bear much fruit (John 15:8). Moses made Israel aware that it was "God who gave them the ability [power] to gain Wealth" (Deut. 8:18). And how will the Lord give them that ability? "God will bless whatever you put your hand to…" (Deut. 28:8).

The second part of the Genesis Commission was "To Multiply" (Gen. 1:28). **Multiplying refers to our affecting future generations and living in a divine increase.** Jacob increased exceedingly (Gen. 30:43). The children of Israel were fruitful and increased abundantly and multiplied (Ex 1:7). "You shall increase mightily" (Deut. 6:3), for "the Lord shall increase you more and more" (Ps. 115:4).

The third part of the Genesis Commission is when God commanded them to "Fill the Earth!" (Gen. 1:28). "Fill" is used 250 times in the Old Testament and means to bring something to completion or fullness. It instructs all of us to reach our "full potential." The Earth was without form and void until God spent three days forming and four days "filling" the Earth. The Hebrew word for "fill" is "malloy", meaning to endow and consecrate. This word is used in commissioning Aaron and sons to serve as priests before the Lord! God not only has an occupation for you, but a spiritual vocation for you to fulfill upon the Earth.

The last part of the Genesis Commission is to "Subdue the Earth" (Gen. 1:28). To subdue the world within us (I Cor. 9:27), and around us (Heb. 11:33), **let's take the Genesis Commission and create collaborative Wealth to multiply ministry.**

Need, Greed or Seed?

Robert Morris, in his book entitled *The Blessed Life*, informs us that Jesus spent 30% of his time teaching on money. He points out three uses for our money. It can be used to supply our basic Needs. It can be abused when consumed upon "Greed." But its highest use is when it is **GIVEN as "Seed."**

> *"Now He who supplies seed to the sower and bread for food will also supply and multiply your store of seed and will enlarge the harvest of your righteousness."* 2 Cor. 9:10-11.

God is the only one who can supply both our needs and our seed. Kingdom Economics therefore, begins with a different paradigm! The world says, "Get all you can, and can all you get." But Kingdom Economics begins with sowing. "Remember this: Whosoever sows sparingly will also reap sparingly and whosoever sows generously will also reap generously" (2 Cor. 9:6).

There are three laws of Kingdom sowing and reaping:

> **First, "You Reap What You Sow."** You must understand that the genetic factors within the seed determine the crop you will raise. God made each seed to reproduce after its own kind (Gen. 1:11-12). If you sow corn, you're going to reap corn. If you sow into money, you're going to reap money.

You must also understand the environment, the seasons and conditions necessary to sustain life and bring growth. Minnesota is not the best environment for a banana harvest. **We must recognize the best areas to invest and develop Kingdom Wealth.**

The Second law of sowing and reaping is that, "You Reap After You Sow." Genesis 8:22 states "as long as the Earth endures, seedtime and harvest, cold and heat, summer and winter, day and night will never cease." Imagine a foolish farmer waiting on a harvest to come in when he never planted a seed. Interaction must take place between the seed and the soil in order to reap a harvest. After the farmer sows the seed, he must keep the birds from stealing the seed, water the seed, and dig the stones out of the soil that would choke the seed. You can have the biggest bible, but if you don't interact with the word in your heart, it can't produce a harvest. (Our role as Sub-Creators.)

Third and finally "<u>You Reap More Than You Sow</u>." "This is what the Kingdom of God is like. A man scatters seed on the ground. Night and day, whether he sleeps or gets up, the seed sprouts and grows; all by itself the seed produces grain – first the stalk, then the head, then the full kernel" (Mark 4:26-28). A couple of kernels of corn planted as seed will produce a stalk with several ears. Each ear can contain hundreds of kernels (403, on average). **Isn't it time you benefited from Kingdom Economics?** Ⓜ

---

[2]Several research items for this book were found at www.wikipedia. com, no attempt was made to confirm their accuracy beyond that.

Chapter 4: Worldly Economics – By Division

Currency by design is "divisible." Currency is created by man and is of the World Economic System (Matt. 22 17-21).

For this book, we ask you to accept that there are two distinct systems of economics: **the World System** and **the Kingdom of God System**. The title of this book; *Why Divide When You Can Multiply?*, is derived on the very difference between these two systems. We will discuss in detail the Kingdom System in Chapter 6, but for now let's take an even deeper look at our current World Economic System.

In Chapter 3, we discovered the difference between 1) Wealth, 2) Assets, and 3) Currency (Money). The World System works with Currency and Assets and is under the authority of Satan and his principalities and powers (Mammon). In Matthew 6:24, we are told that we cannot serve two masters… You cannot serve God and Mammon.

There are other idols besides Currency that Mammon used to capture our hearts; they are:

Ⓜ**American Idols**
"American Idol" is a reality television singing competition based on the UK show "Pop Idol." After its debut in 2002, it has become one of the most popular shows in the history of American television. As of 2011, it was the most watched TV series in Nielson Ratings and the only program to be #1 for seven consecutive seasons.

Joshua 24:2 sadly tells us that, "…they served other gods…" An idol is anything or anyone that is loved or admired to an excessive degree:

An object of infatuation. Clearly America is infatuated with money and many idols. Psalm 78:58, informs us of how Israel "Moved Him to jealousy with their graven images." The Greek word for image refers to a tool for engraving. Being exposed to over 1,500 secular commercial messages a day on average, it's no wonder that we have the world's economic philosophy engraved in us.

Call of Duty
Within 24 hours of going on sale, "Call of Duty: Blacks Ops," sold more than 5.6 million copies. The video game portrays "foot soldiers" confronting the enemy in obedience to their "call of duty." We too have been "called of duty" to combat the "dark ops" of the enemy and remove his occupation of God's territory. Note the 8 P's of the enemy's plan to bring us into bondage.

The P's: Non-Money Worldly Desires:
1. **Pleasure.** The world's currency will not bring true Wealth or happiness. Solomon had an annual income of more than $25 million. He lived in a palace that it took 13 years to build. He owned 40,000 horses, sat on an ivory throne overlaid with gold, but said, "He who loves money will never have enough. It is foolish to think that money brings happiness. The more you have, the more you spend, right up to the limits of your income" (Ecc. 5:10-11).

2. **Profane.** Satan is a master counterfeiter (2 Cor. 11:3). He profanes God-ordained true Wealth with perversions. Consider our "Bull" on Wall Street. It refers back to the ancient golden calf and Egyptian god of prosperity. The unfinished pyramid on our dollar bill points to the unfinished tower of Babel symbolizing satanic rebellion. Some say the all-seeing eye was a symbol of God's providence, while others maintain that it is the unseen force of Babylon watching over the completion of the evil kingdom. The Illuminati, founded by Adam Weishoupt in 1776, spread their poison through free-masonry which has a communist agenda. Obelisks

like the Washington Monument are symbols of ancient promiscuity and the worship of the male sexual organ and man's ability to procreate rather than God's ability to create all life. Even our Statue of Liberty mimics the design of ancient goddesses such as Diana in Ephesus, Isis in Egypt and Ishtar in Babylon! Ⓜ

3. **Power.** Since the beginning of time, men have sought power and control from a small group. This is the primary reason most of the world systems of government and business are failing. We have made Power an idol to be worshiped.

4. **Prestige.** Keeping up with the Jones, lusting for what another has, and selling our soul to get it has brought much destruction. The Bible says, if you exalt yourself you will be abased and if you humble yourself you will be lifted up. Where most people get confused is in the meaning of humble. This does not mean poor and without power or purpose.

5. **Possessions.** A famous bumper sticker says, "He who dies with the most toys wins!" What a lie that is. If you make possessions your god, when you die you are just dead since you can't take it with you.

6. **Payday or Pension.** Somehow we have been conditioned to believe that it is our efforts which make us successful absent from the favor of God. What a mistake this is. Retirement – what a concept – there is no retirement in the Bible. Retirement is a World Economic System ideal. It is not in the Bible.

7. **Position.** Having the title or being the big man on campus leads to a pursuit of Glory and that always ends poorly. Look at how many CEOs, politicians and others are in prison today thinking "they were all that and a bag of chips."

8. **Privilege.** This is maybe one of the worst affecting our younger generation. They have seen the prosperity of their

parents and they are not willing to go through the process of gaining experience before taking on success. They want to all start as the boss or a manager. Consider Luke 12: 22-26, Then turning to his disciples, Jesus said, "So I tell you, don't worry about everyday life -- whether you have enough food to eat or clothes to wear. For life consists of far more than food and clothing. Look at the ravens. They don't need to plant or harvest or put food in barns because God feeds them. And you are far more valuable to him than any birds! Can all your worries add a single moment to your life? Of course not! And if worry can't do little things like that, what's the use of worrying over bigger things?"

Four Economic Sectors

The World Economic System by its method of operation brings about Division. There are four economic sectors we will discuss for the rest of this book; they are:

1. **Public:** meaning a system of government or governance (laws and rules).

2. **Private:** meaning a for-profit system in its structure.

3. **Social:** meaning a non-government, likely non-profit system in its structure.

4. **Cooperative:** meaning a democratic mutual system of governance using either for-profit or non-profit systems in its structure.

"The first three sectors (Public, Private and Social) centralize power in the hands of a few with a goal to control or govern the masses. The fourth sector, Cooperative, is a mutual democratic system of governance where each member has an equal vote.

We believe that Cooperative is the system that will support the emergence of the Kingdom Economic System model based in multiplication."

The Cycles of Power

In Chapter 1: The Cycle of Power and Revolution, of *Wealth 3.0 – Saving America One Small Business At A Time*, I discussed the thesis was "Someone To Watch Over Me!" Here is an excerpt:

> *Throughout history, when a people would seek to create a society, they would raise up a leader to establish the rules for the society to operate or a leader would rise and establish a set of rules that define that society.*
>
> *The majority of humans are as sheep among wolves; they need someone to watch over them and protect them from things that go bump in the night. This has given rise to typically a leader from the people who is driven or inspired to help the people achieve a set of societal goals. Often this first leader will grow weary and appoint a system of judges to help enforce the new societal rules or the leader will become a King and take absolute power over the people. This King will receive the approval of the people and as the King will provide structure, food, protection, and a system of justice.*

This led me to understand how society changes through cycles and I provided this chart below as figure 1: The Cycle of Power and Revolution.

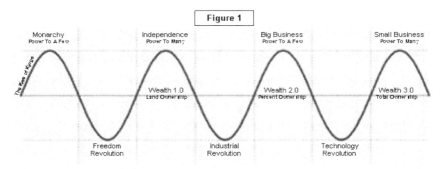

In the United States today, we are at the point of change of cycle where what I call Wealth 3.0 will occur and "power will move into the hands of many." **If we conduct a peaceful revolution, it will be a new structure of governance created from the best of a republic + democracy + capitalism + cooperative (A Collaborative Commonwealth).** In the next section, "Centralize Power: Public," we will define all these systems.

We have lived under the strong Fear of terrorism since 2001. We have suffered at the expense of life and capital in long wars. We have seen corruption in our political Kings and their administrations who have dealt away our freedoms. Now, we want someone to rise up and make it all better – "we want someone powerful to watch over us!" There is a better plan, where we take control of our individual lives while collaborating on key social issues and needs. Let's look at a quote I included in my book *Wealth 3.0.*

> **Consider this quote:** *"A democracy cannot exist as a permanent form of government. It can only exist until the voters discover that they can vote themselves largesse from the public treasury. From that moment on, the majority always votes for the candidates promising the most benefits from the public treasury with the result that a democracy always collapses over loose fiscal policy,*

always followed by a dictatorship. The average age of the world's greatest civilizations has been 200 years.

Great nations rise and fall. The people go from bondage to spiritual truth, to great courage, from courage to liberty, from liberty to abundance, from abundance to selfishness, from selfishness to complacency, from complacency to apathy, from apathy to dependence, from dependence back again to bondage." - ALEXANDER FRASER TYTLER (1747 – 1813). **Some researchers disagree that Tytler authored this entire quote. Either way, the quote merits our consideration today.**

Spiritual Déjà Vu

First Corinthians 15:46, informs us that, "first the natural, then the spiritual." Tytler's Fatal Sequence has a spiritual dimension as well. The Old Testament book of Judges reveals the spiritual reasons for their physical realities. Israel's bondage cycle begins with sin. This brings them into Servitude (national bondage). Servitude inspired Supplication (calling upon God). Spiritual renewal brought about their Salvation (national deliverance). But unfortunately, Salvation led them to Self-Sufficiency apart from God and into Sin.

Seem familiar? When I wrote *Wealth 3.0*, I was considering that **the next revolution would cause an emergence of "small business" that would place wealth back in the hands of many.** At that time, I had not considered both economic systems and today I believe that small business will emerge, but it will be in a collaborative social network likely connected by a system of cooperatives (4th Sector), a federation of Collaborative Commonwealths. The revolution is not far away, we are already seeing movements of young people (i.e. Occupy Wall Street).

Who will emerge as leadership? Is this the right direction for our youth or are they pawns for Mammon's plan?

> *"This struggle must be organized, according to "all the rules of the art", by people who are professionally engaged in revolutionary activity. The fact that the masses are spontaneously being drawn into the movement does not make the organization of this struggle* less necessary. *On the contrary, it makes it* more necessary" - *Lenin*

From Chapter 3, we learned, Wealth is not a man thing, but a God thing. The best man can do is earn Percentage Increase on his Assets. God can multiply 30, 60, and 100 fold in the same timeframe!

Let's review and you will see why I believe the "fragile" nature of these methods will not succeed, even if we choose them. **We need a new "agile" method! Not a failing "fragile" method.**

Centralized Power: Public (Government or Governance)

Forms of Governance, Power & Control	Power in the Hands of Few	Power in the Hands of Many
Republic		X
Democracy	X	
Theocracy *		X
Commonwealth **		X
Fascism	X	
Socialism	X	
Communism	X	
Dictatorship	X	
Capitalism	X	

* A form of sovereign commonwealth with ecclesiastical governance.
** See Collaborative Commonwealth, Chapter 8

Republic. In the United States we are a Republic. A Republic is defined[1] as a state in which the supreme power rests in the body of citizens entitled to vote and is exercised by representatives chosen directly or indirectly by them. Any body of persons viewed as a commonwealth, or a state in which the head of government is neither a monarch, nor other hereditary head of state. We often refer to ourselves as a **Democracy** which is defined[1] as government by the people; a form of government in which the supreme power is vested in the people and exercised directly by them or by their elected agents under a free electoral system. So what is the difference? In **Republics, sovereignty is vested in each citizen, where in a Democracy, sovereignty is vested in the majority of the group.** Some would say that Democracy is a dictatorship of the group versus by an individual. What this really gets down to is individual rights versus group needs.

For each person, **your rights spring forth from your creator, not the worldly government in any form**. As Christians, we acknowledge that ultimately (in the millennial reign) we will operate as a Theocracy. A **Theocracy** is defined[1] as a form of government in which God is recognized as the supreme civil ruler, with God's laws being interpreted by the ecclesiastical authorities (rule and reign) as a commonwealth or state under such a form or system of government. The definition[1] of **Commonwealth,** in order to find clarity, is a group of sovereign states [or individuals as in a Republic] and their dependencies **associated by their own choice and linked with common objectives and interests**.

If the US operated as a Republic (and it should), then we would not see the passing of laws in the middle of the night out of fear and a herd mentality. Instead, we would engage in an open debate protecting the rights of the individual. Frankly, we are seeing our government slip into near-monarchy-like control [dictatorship – see Tytler quote again]. In fact in 2011, in order to minimize debt growth, there was a proposal to create a "Super Congress" made up of six Republicans and six Democrats that would make the rules. Can you see the drawing of power into the hands of a select few? What about the fact there are more than two parties today? We might even ask, "Are there really even two parties today?"

Fascism. Fascism is defined[1] as a governmental system led by a dictator having complete power, forcibly suppressing opposition and criticism, regimenting all industry, commerce, etc., and emphasizing an aggressive nationalism and often racism. How does this relate to the bailouts of those "too big to fail" businesses? Are we nationalizing our banking system? If so, why?

An answer will depend on your views of "fiat currency." Fiat currency is paper money that is not backed by an asset such as gold and silver; rather, it is created out of thin air by a government or central bank action. In 1971, President Nixon established the law that removed the requirement for the US Dollar to be backed by gold. Once this occurred, it created a debtor mindset (see Chapter 5) whereby we have mortgaged our future. This has been compounded by government-backed home loans and student loans and their ultimate securitization which resulted in the bailouts or as it is called in criminal law – a Ponzi scheme. Finally, the surrendering of our personal rights, because we have become fiscally and personally lazy, is simply "someone to watch over me" [review Republic again].

Now I am not saying we are becoming a Fascist state. However, in light of the Tytler Fatal Sequence and current events, we might be sliding into a Dictatorship or One World Government if we don't stand up! Consider the recent riots worldwide and now here in the US; there is social unrest, but is it focused on the problem or simply manipulated to achieve a hidden satanic goal? This is not conspiracy theory; it is prophecy in the news!

> *"Power is not a means, it is an end. One does not establish a dictatorship in order to safeguard a revolution; one makes the revolution in order to establish a dictatorship – George Orwell."*

Socialism/Communism. The definitions[1] are: **Socialism** is a theory or system of social organization that advocates the vesting of the ownership and control of the means of production and distribution, of capital, land, etc., "in the community" as a whole. [On its face, not a bad ideal until you consider the next part.] In Marxist theory, the stage following capitalism in which the society transitions to communism, characterized by the imperfect implementation of collectivist principles. [Collectivist meaning[1], the political principle of centralized social and economic control, especially of all means of production. See Fascism above.] **Communism** is a theory or system of social organization based on the holding of all property in common, actual ownership being ascribed to the community as a whole or to the state, not individuals. Further defined as a system of social organization in which all economic and social activity is controlled by a totalitarian state dominated by a single and self-perpetuating political party. [Or Super Congress?]

Again, I am not saying that we are becoming a Communist nation. I think those are 20th Century concepts which have been replaced with a new [world] order established in Crisis as we discussed in Chapter 2.

Dictatorships. Dictatorships are defined[1] as a country, government, or the form of government in which absolute power is exercised by a dictator [either one person or a small elite group like a Super Congress].

We are not currently a dictatorship, but our national sovereignty and our personal sovereignty are at risk; I am sure you will agree. In business we are subject to a hostile takeover by our debtors which are nations that have Fascist, Socialist, Communist, and Dictator leaders at their helm. Do I think this will happen in the US? Likely not. But I do believe we will see consolidations, much like in business. It is not a far stretch to see a North American Union made up of Mexico, the United States, and Canada. Recent news has reported a number of nations moving toward economic unions because of the global financial crisis. Mammon is at work carrying out the plan of his god, Satan. This may be the beginning of the formation of the 10 world unions that will make up the One World Government. (Ref: *En Route to Global Occupation*, by Gary Kah, page 40 – Club of Rome)

1. NAFTA (America, Canada and Mexico)
2. The E.U. – Countries of the European Union, Western Europe as a whole
3. Japan
4. Australia, New Zealand, South Africa
5. Eastern Europe, Pakistan, Afghanistan, Russia and the former countries of the Soviet Union
6. Central and South America, Cuba and Caribbean Islands
7. The Middle East and North Africa
8. The rest of Africa, except South Africa
9. South and Southeast Asia, including India
10. China (Mongolia is now included with China)

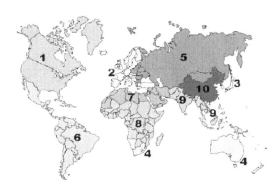

Centralized Power: Private

For our discussions, we considered the Private Sector to be all for-profit organizations, but it is so large that we cannot discuss every industry. For the purposes of this book, we have limited it to the financial industry and specifically Banking, Wall Street and the Real Estate crisis. Let's first begin with an understanding of Capitalism which is the cornerstone of American business and is certainly on the endangered species list.

Capitalism. Capitalism is defined[1] as an economic system in which investment in and ownership of **the means of production, distribution, and exchange of wealth [assets and currency] is made and maintained chiefly by private individuals or corporations, especially as contrasted to cooperatively or state-owned means** of wealth [Capital]. It is easy to forget that Capitalism was coined not so long ago, in the mid-19th century, when the Industrial Revolution was in full swing and individual entrepreneurs were creating new industries and amassing wealth [Assets]. Terms for the other two major competing economic systems of the past two centuries—Socialism and Communism—were also coined around the same time. Many people fiercely espouse Capitalism as an economic freedom inseparable from democracy [or do they mean Republic?], as reflected in several books considered classics and still avidly read today: for example, *Capitalism and Freedom* by Nobel laureate Milton Friedman (1962), and *Capitalism, Socialism and Democracy* by Joseph A. Schumpeter (1943).

I am sure you will agree clearly that words and their meanings matter. I know this is a tough chapter with all these definitions, but without them we would not have a common language to communicate the new concepts coming in the next chapters. The Bible says that words matter [Proverbs 18:21] even unto life and death.

In my book, *Is There Life After Debt?* (1990), I discussed the financial system; here are some of the excerpts from that book (indented and in italics). I have made my current comments intermingled with this text in brackets [...]. I trust this will help you follow my thought process and will be consistent throughout this book.

> *Where did it all begin? Was financial bondage always a part of American life or was there really a time when people lived outside the fear of credit and creditors? The roots of the American Financial System can be found in the early 1900's.*

> ### The Great Depression

> *The Great Depression ranks as one of the worst business slumps, and included the longest period of high unemployment and lowest business activity in modern times.* [Until now?]

> *In October 1929 President Herbert Hoover watched as stock prices plummeted, sending thousands of investors into poverty and many more still into total financial collapse. Banks and stores closed, families lost their homes in foreclosure, and Americans found themselves broke and jobless.* [Sound like 2009 and beyond?]

> *The years preceding the "crash" saw the stock market reach new highs, as the price of common stocks doubled between 1925 and 1929.* [Sound like the 1990's?]

Middle Class American workers were lured to the market, hoping to duplicate the newly increased prosperity of fellow workers. Those who purchased early reaped large benefits, only to be sucked deeper into the system, speculating on questionable stocks, hoping to make large profits following future increases. [Sound like 2008 and beyond?]

Stock prices dropped rapidly on October 24, 1929 (better known as Black Thursday). A selling frenzy hit the floor of the New York Stock Exchange as over 11,000,000 shares traded in a single afternoon. Speculation was that the bankers had caused the sudden sell-off, waiting like vultures for their victims to bleed to death and take advantage of the lower prices. Knowing that the market had lost over $100 million in equity in one week, the manipulators of the market could call the margin accounts (those who had bought on credit could be forced to sell early to raise the money to re-pay the loan that was being called), forcing the small investors to sell in a down market, manipulating prices even lower. The larger investors could then purchase their original holdings and profit when the stocks regained value. [Were we manipulated again, but this time to steal our pensions, home equity and job security? If you have not seen the movie called *Too Big To Fail*, it is a must see to understand the culture and times in which we live.]

Margin Accounts [Today, they used Credit Default Swaps]

The average American sat on the sidelines as the large banks and merchants made large profits in the stock market. [Since the collapse in 2009, the Banks have made record profits on money loaned to them by our government.]

Much like the Gold Rush in California during the period of expansion, small investors rushed to the stock market hoping to "strike it rich" like the big boys. These investors did not have the liquidity of the larger players, but were lured into the market through a system called margin accounts. These accounts allowed the smaller investors to place down as little as 10% of the price, borrowing the balance from the banker or broker. The system would allow a smaller investor to "play the market" and pay the loan from excess profits made when the stock prices rose. The plan seemed logical and past performance of the market virtually assured success. (Sound familiar?)

The 40 and 80 Year Economic Cycles

How is this time different? The banking system and mortgage companies got every American who could fog a mirror to buy one or more homes on stated income so they could feed the demand for hedge funds and other global investors to earn above average yields on the securitization pools of mortgages, car loans, credit cards, and student loans. Wall Street backed this securitization with insurance on the pool, leading the investors to believe they could not lose. All the while the plan was to steal trillions of dollars of our national net worth with undisclosed fees, commissions and profit-taking. [Was 2009 similar to 1929, just "80 years" later? See the chart that follows.]

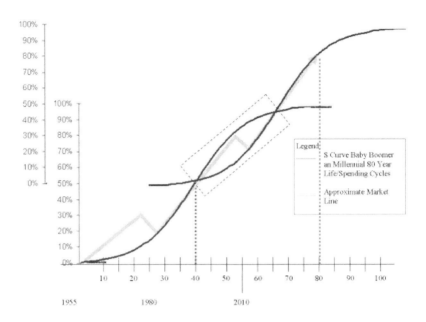

Now I am a businessman and there is nothing wrong with a profit, but when it destroys everyone, the consumer and investor alike, it is wrong. Fortunately at the end of 2011, after much complaining by consumers and investors alike, the Ponzi scheme is about to come apart.

My S-curve chart which tracks the 40 and 80 year cycles of our economy relative to the Baby Boomers and their children (the Millennials). I predict that we will see the collapse of most of the major banks and Wall Street firms by the end of 2013 maybe earlier. Further I predict, if we work hard, we can correct this theft and begin the return to normal as early as 2016 without anymore bailout interference. This chart has been an amazing predictor of the future; not because I am such a great analyst, but because Mammon's underlying plan has not changed for over 250 years.

Harry S. Dent, Jr., in his book, *The Great Depression Ahead – How to Prosper in the Debt Crisis of 2010-2012,* predicts we will not see our economy recover until 2023. Certainly, Mr. Dent has a better track record than I at such predictions. I am optimistic; he is less optimistic;

so maybe we are both wrong and the recovery will occur somewhere in between. What I know is, if we keep on the current path, there may not even be a recovery.

As you can see by the words from my earlier book, we could predict it then (1990). It really doesn't matter what the leadership tells us, Republican or Democrat; Mammon's plan continues to move forward!

Let's just look at a little more from *Is There Life After Debt?*.

> *In a time when mortgages on homes were rare and car loans lasted no longer than 12 months, bankers were respected, conservative members of society and the only credit most used was at the local grocer, the economy was turned upside down, screaming for government protection and support.* [Sounds like today as well]

> ### *Roosevelt And The New Deal*

> *This economy was ripe for promises of a "brighter tomorrow" and a quick fix from the government, even if it meant "signing over their children's future."* [Have we not heard very similar words from President Obama?]

> *This is the American Economy that elected Franklin D. Roosevelt in 1932. Educated at Harvard and a follower of economist Dr. John Maynard Keynes (a proclaimed socialist and believer that the government should control banking and business to assure prosperity), Roosevelt offered a "NEW DEAL" to a country crying out for government assistance.*

> [President Obama has been highly criticized about having advisors who are Socialist. It is true that history

repeats itself, or a winning team keeps running its trick play until the other side (us) learns and puts up a proper defense (kick them out!)]

Human suffering in the United States rose to a new high. Over 25% of the population was out of work.

[Only about 10% with the new math of today, but we are not counting those who have taken a job at lesser pay to survive and the college students who can't find a job. What else are they not telling us?]

The short-sighted desire for a "quick fix" traded freedom for government control. Roosevelt's "a chicken in every pot" slogan offered government assistance for a floundering economy while stealing prosperity for generations to come.

[Today it is called Quantitative Easing. Same game, different words!]

In a special session of Congress, called THE HUNDRED DAYS, laws were passed to relieve the depression. This program was called the NEW DEAL and the goal was to institute government control through implementation of several key agenda items.

[Since 2009, we have ObamaCare, and a dozen other bills no one has read! To quote our leadership, "never miss a good crisis to get something through..."]

"A democracy is not a form of government to survive. For

it will only succeed until its citizens discover they can vote themselves money

*from the treasury, then they will bankrupt
it."* **Karl Marx**

[Seems everyone agrees with Tytler!]

*... the creation of a CENTRAL BANKING SYSTEM
allowed the government the power to increase or
decrease the money supply, control labor costs, and
control inflation.* [For more information – Google about
the Bretton Woods Convention of July 1944]

*...the development of the Federal Deposit Insurance
Corporation drew banks into the Centralized Banking
System like flies to sugar. This allowed the government
(and the private "Federal Reserve System") final and
total control of the banking industry and management of
the monetary system, assuring total compliance through
its member banks.*

[This time it was "billions in bailout loans" and "the
new $250,000 FDIC limit" or they would shut your bank
down. What will really happen when all the banks are
forced to come clean on the real value of the real estate
portfolios? Most will be insolvent and I don't think the
American people will accept another bailout, do you?
Consider, is this the right time to attempt to change
America's form or government?]

*... The interest payments on the National Debt now
consume 17% of total tax revenues. This figure is
expected to jump to 500% of all tax revenues by the year
2000.*

We are now at $15 Trillion and climbing. Isn't it amazing, that when I
wrote *Is There Life After Debt?* (20 years ago) that nothing has changed.
Nothing will change until we either change Mammon's system or the
Lord returns. Even so, come Lord Jesus!

We can leave behind a remnant of Kingdom Economic principles that the world can rebuild on in the Millennial Age. **Is this part of your calling or assignment? Go to www.wdwycm.com.**

Banking. We have predicted huge bank failures due to devaluation of the bank asset portfolios' toxic assets. If the banks can legally overcome this problem, there remains yet another looming problem. Several states attorneys' general, the FBI, and other government (state and federal) alphabet groups are investigating this corruption. Groups like American HomeOwners Cooperative (AmericanHomeownersCoOp.com) and blogs similar to LivingLies Blog (LivingLies.wordpress.com) have led the way to get consumers and investors alike to stand up for their rights as citizens and not be pawns in this financial Ponzi scheme created by the banking, mortgage and Wall Street firms whom I believe are under the demonic influence of Mammon.

Wall Street. In addition to complicity in the securitization fraud on America, Wall Street has other problems. Citizens are staging protests like Occupy Wall Street and at other Occupy sites all over the country. The fragile models of most businesses that have little to no working capital are failing daily. This is leaving Wall Street brokers with buyers departing from traditional securities (stocks, bonds, and mutual funds) and investing in commodities such as gold and silver. Finally, if that was not enough, there will be litigation over pension fund fiduciary conflicts of interest from pension fund managers and consumers who have lost money while these Wall Street firms have plundered the opportunities with unconscionable fees.

I know these words are tough, but in the next 24 to 36 months, they will become normal headlines. I have sources in media and government that have confirmed prosecution and bad press are about to be unleashed as early as second quarter 2012. Further, there are law firms I have spoken to or who have been relayed to me by my sources that are already preparing lawsuits. It is estimated that it may take 20 years to clear this litigation in the courts.

Again, it begins with the securitization issues, but the stock market as we know it as well as many other financial institutions will be forever changed and weakened for lack of trust.

Real Estate. Maybe the biggest issue here is the more than 100 Million mortgage transactions (including refinance deals) that occurred in the last 10 years or so. What we have discovered is that the overall valuation of the properties was overstated causing millions of loan modifications to be required; some markets have lost 30 to 70% of their value. The once stable and totally reliable mortgage industry and its loan process has forever been corrupted and will require a massive overhaul to build any trust in the future.

If this was a typical market, (and it is anything but typical), the pressures of capitalism would naturally cure this problem in about four years time. Losses would be written off and new profits taken and it would balance out. It is like the stock market; every time there is a winner, there has to be a loser to keep it in balance.

One major problem is, when this beast was created to feed the demands of Wall Street, everyone got sloppy with the paperwork. Often there was no paperwork available and if it is available now, my sources can prove most of it is fraudulent and likely created after the fact. Moreover, the Deed of Trust (mortgage) has been separated from the Title which clouds the title every time.

Even if the average American did not participate in this scam and really just bought a home to live in, gave accurate personal information, got a real appraisal, and really just qualified for the mortgage, when that mortgage was sold into the financial markets by banks and Wall Street, the pools disconnected the lender from the buyer in violation of almost every real estate legislation (i.e. RESPA). **I hope you got what I just said; there are potentially over 100 million real estate transactions that are messed up, representing trillions of dollars in real estate and investor dollars.** That's right; both sides of the title transaction are messed up. Who lent, who borrowed, who owns the note all totally messed up, but the banks and Wall Street got bailouts and insurance money so they are making record profits in the process while America and the world suffer.

Truthfully, many foreclosures are likely fraudulent too; many home sales are fraudulent; it is a real mess. My real estate contacts tell me that Realtors® are being asked to verify the Title is valid; how can they do that? They are just being made scapegoats too.

Even consumers, who are just selling their homes for a variety of good reasons, cannot be assured by title companies, if their loan was securitized, that their title is clear and without defect. In fact, if you read your title policy, likely they have released themselves of that liability if your loan was securitized and they did not inform you at closing. It's no wonder that title companies are folding all over America.

My concern is, will this lead to new legislation, since the government owns the majority of the mortgages, to nationalize all real estate in an attempt to clear title? [Re-read the definition of Communism] Is this Mammon's plan to take our homes? Commercial real estate has the same problems! Will this lead to a Fascist-like system or even a Communist-like government or will we become the North American Union and lose our personal and national sovereignty? Will this destroy the US Dollar as the world's reserve currency? These are serious questions, yet the average American sits at home watching sports and sitcoms. The same was true when the Roman Empire fell; they attended the Circus and watched Christians and slaves die in battle and just laughed until their nation was no more. Revelation is being revealed!

Centralized Power: Social

The Social Sector, unlike the previous two, is for the so called non-profit organizations. In my recent White Paper entitled, *The Decline of the*

Non-Profit Organization (NPO), I took a look at why these organizations are experiencing a decline in support (giving).

According to the Urban Institute (2009), [for NPOs] "major funding sources have fewer resources and revenues have declined." The Bridgespan Group reports, "Non-profits are turning to much tougher measures... to cope with the economic downturn."

Facts: 35% have reduced budgets

43% have or will use their reserves

50% have reduced travel

36% have reduced training

41% have cut staff

37% have frozen hiring

26% have cut wages

39% have cut programs

What is becoming an even more significant challenge to NPOs is the ability to find, keep, and motivate the right talent. It is expected that as many as 75% of Executive Directors will leave their organizations by the end of 2013. Nearly half of the younger professionals say they will have to leave, according to John Schetzer, in *The Future of the Non-profit Sector.* This is likely due to the need for more income, lack of training, and commercial opportunities.

The Church. According to The Barna Group, "During the first five years of the decade, an average of 84 cents out of every dollar donated by born-again adults went to churches. In the past three years, though, the proportion has declined to just 76 cents out of every donated dollar."

IMPACT OF THE POOR ECONOMY: AMERICANS DROP DONATIONS

LAST THREE MONTHS	Nov 2008	Jan 2010
% of adults who have reduced giving to non-profits*	31%	48%
% of adults who have reduced giving to churches	20%	29%

* excludes churches(Source: The Barna Group, Ventura, CA - OmniPoll^{SM} 2010, N=1,008)

LifeWay Research indicates "**about 5% of the average church budget goes to missions and evangelism**."

While some church organizations see an increase in giving, most churches have not. Those seeing donations increase have incorporated Web 2.0 and social media techniques to expand the base of donors. Why is this necessary?

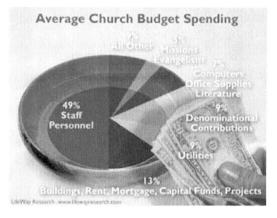

The donor is either frustrated with the integrity of the organization's ability to serve its mission statement or frustrated from wasteful spending.

This is evidenced by only 5% of donations getting to those in need (in this case Missions and Evangelism) while staff costs can consume up to 49%. (See Average Church Budget Spending Chart at www. lifewayresearch.com).

It is my experience, that the traditional Donor Model is broken. Moreover, as governments seek sources of additional revenue, the tax deduction for gifts is in jeopardy. This means that either the government will stop the deduction or they may claim control over NPOs budgets because they have provided deductions in the past. The days of the government partnering with religious and social causes are likely over. In order for government to maintain its power, it must enlarge its revenue to meet certain social demands of its population (seeking so-called social change or social justice). **How long will it be before we nationalize charities and remove the tax deduction for giving to churches?**

The Marketplace. There are two major areas I considered; the first is the traditional non-religious NPO and the free social network.

The **traditional non-religious NPO** is varied in mission. Nearly every cause has an organization that is seeking to raise money for its affinity. Fundraising comes in two forms: 1) annual budget and 2) endowment. Despite the facts mentioned at the first of this section, NPOs do receive funding from other foundations and certain governmental programs, usually in the form of grants. The real secret to funding NPO activity is grant writing, unless you can become a nationally-known program.

Nationally-known programs such as Jerry's Kids (The MDA Telethon) are able to raise annual budgets using retail campaigns and the media. Breast Cancer awareness and its pink ribbon has also met with above-average success. However, local programs suffer from a lack of funding for the annual budget and almost never raise enough to start an endowment. On the other hand, many colleges and universities have become excellent raisers of endowment capital working through their graduates as a social network. The secret is how do you create a social network? **However, student loans were securitized too. What happens as students who can't get jobs default on these loans and colleges and universities can't get this money to meet their budgets? Without a change, I predict a failure in the education system as early as 2016.**

The free social networks such as Facebook, Twitter, Linked-In, etc. are for-profits that are similar to NPOs in that many don't make a profit unless they have determined how to monetize the advertising revenue potential of their participants. There is an entire genre of websites that emerged out of the dot-bomb era that offer the services of their website free to users. These websites create such social culture surrounding FREE that if you then try and monetize them with advertising, the participants often threaten to flee. However, websites such as Facebook and even YouTube are breaking through and beginning to earn revenue. Other websites, for example dating websites, actually charge a membership ·fee and provide social interaction. I have mentioned these organizations here, because I believe they are the forerunners of new concepts on the rise which I will discuss in Chapter 8.

The Unions Are Making A Comeback. Generally, labor unions in America are legally recognized as representatives of workers in a wide variety of industries. In the beginning, labor unions were created to overcome some serious issues related to workers such as child labor abuses, excessive hours in a work week, employee benefits, and employee rights defense.

Coming into prominence in the 1800's, many unions developed quickly and several unions failed due to poor organization. By the early 1900's unions began to re-emerge in support of the Democratic agenda and as a result of the Wagner Act. By the 1950's the Taft-Hartley Act and talk of corruption in organizations like the Teamsters, caused the popularity of Unions to fade.

Today, unions are trying to make another comeback (as a social network) in the name of "people power" still following a Democratic agenda -- some would say a Socialist agenda. One of the most publicized of these, the Association of Community Organizations for Reform Now (ACORN), had favor with Congress until a conservative investigative report in 2009 caused a repeal of their funding. While ACORN was not a labor union per se, they were a **labor and community development movement**. Many of their activities were developed around excellent causes such as predatory lending practices, Katrina relief, voter education, wages, and gun control. However, much like the issues with the Teamsters, in the 1950's, corruption was their downfall.

ACORN had over 30 state chapters, was in more than 100 cities, in over 1200 communities and had over 400,000 members. Properly managed, it would have been an excellent movement serving people.

However, like all the organizations in this chapter, there was still the work of the World System drawing power back to a limited number of leaders who fell to Satan's plan of Absolute Power Corrupts! **I call it the 3-G's -- either Gold, Glory, and Girls. Most great leaders fall for one or more of these three corrupting powers.**

Chapter 5: Debt As A Lever

Already we have discussed debt and its impact on society. In this chapter, we are going to look at Debt As A Lever. Debt is defined[1] as something that is owed or that one is bound to pay or perform for another. In the Bible, debt is an offense requiring reparation; a sin; a trespass. Reparation is defined[1] as the making of amends for wrong or injury done. A Lever is defined[1] in mechanics as a rigid bar that pivots about one point and that is used to move an object at a second point by a force applied at a third. A Lever is further defined[1] as a means or agency of persuading or of achieving an end. **A restatement of the definitions above relative to Debt As A Lever: a way Satan uses the love of money as his agent to cause us to trust money more than God and therefore fall into sin.**

The Central Banking System
Several years ago, our Central Bank (the Federal Reserve, which is neither Federal nor a reserve, but a private corporation acting as a bank) published a document entitled *Modern Money Mechanics* (a Lever) which describes the fractional reserve banking system or fiat currency (Division).

First the Federal Reserve Banking System (the Fed) as Central Bank wants to issue money so it gets the US Government (really any government) to issue bonds from which the Fed creates its own notes (Federal Reserve Note – a debt, called the dollar). Once deposited in a bank, it becomes currency (see Chapter 3) in our U.S. Money Supply. Interesting is that today only 3% of currency actually gets printed into physical dollars to be used by "we the people" and 97% is in an electronic digital form. Hence, Currency = Debt! So what we are really talking about is Currency As A Lever. Said another way, Satan is using Currency, the mechanics of money as the way (a Lever) he gets us to trust him more than God's Wealth which by its nature is free.

All deposits become bank assets. Your savings, bonds, IRAs, pensions, mortgages, etc. are all counted as "the bank's" assets. The bank is required to "reserve" about 10% of these assets according to *Modern Money Mechanics*. This leaves 90% which is called the "excess reserve" and can be the basis for new loans (more Currency).

What this really means is that the 90% is freed up to create loan contracts. When the proceeds of the loan contracts are deposited in a bank to pay bills or buy a car, the bank gets to call that an asset too. Since the bank's assets have increased (not), then they can loan 90% of the 90% or 81% and so on to infinity; there is no real limit!

As banks continue to loan currency this way the dollars devalue through a thing called "inflation" which is widely accepted as the hidden tax we pay to enable this private corporation called the Fed to operate our banking system. This devaluation represents that $1 in 1913 requires $21.60 in 2007 to have the same spending power. Have your parents ever asked you what you do with all your money? You see when they bought their homes, for example, they locked that price in the inflation of 20 years ago; homes cost more now simply because of this lending cycle which creates inflation.

Said another way, our now over $15 Trillion in national debt is equal basically to the Money Supply. If we stopped borrowing there wouldn't be fiat currency and the dollar would collapse!

The Impact of Debt with Interest
Interest is not in the Money Supply as there is no debt to create Currency. **This is why to balance the scales, bankruptcy and foreclosure exist. Was this the reason that we have seen all the recent foreclosures; was it the way to balance the scales?** In 1969, in a famous Minnesota

court case, Jerome Daily argued that since the bank created the Currency for his loan out of the air the bank did not really exchange anything, therefore making the note invalid. Mr. Daily won his case! In the judge's ruling he states, "… only God can create something out of nothing…"

Consider the mortgage crisis and the ultimate securitization of that debt. It goes something like this; we borrowed money the banks did not have (electric money) which they created out of thin air and the bank can charge interest and fees they don't deserve; then the banks get money for those notes from Wall Street (from our pensions and savings) for these loans. The Wall Street firms then earn big fees and commissions and cover that with insurance on firms "we the people" bail out. We work hard to pay debts that don't exist to banks that did not have the money who then are using our pensions to make more Currency that we borrow and work our lives to repay as credit card, car, consumer and education loans. All of course are then backed in one way or another by our government (which is really our willingness to pay). **We are paying more than twice for money that doesn't exist with our labor. We have become slaves to the money god. Mammon has us in bondage.**

Physical slavery requires people to be housed and fed. Economic slavery requires people to feed themselves and house themselves.

What Our Founders Had To Say
Let's look at some comments from our founders which Hal Lindsey covered on his TV show The Hal Lindsey Report:

"Let me issue and control a nation's money and I care not who writes its laws." Mayer Rothschild, creator of the Central Bank.

"If the people ever allow the banks to issue their currency, the banks and corporations which will grow up around them will deprive the people of all property, until their children wake up homeless on the continent their fathers conquered." President Thomas Jefferson.

"History records that the money changers have used every form of abuse, intrigue, deceit, and violent means possible, to maintain their control over governments, by controlling money and its issuance."
President James Madison

"If Congress has the right under the Constitution to issue paper money, it was given to them to use themselves, not to be delegated to individuals or corporations." President Andrew Jackson

"The 'money powers' prey on the nation in times of peace and conspire against it in times of adversity. The banking powers are more despotic than monarchy, more insolent than autocracy, more selfish than bureaucracy. They denounce as public enemies all who question their methods or throw light upon their crimes. I have two great enemies, the Southern Army in the front of me, and the bankers in the rear. Of the two, the one at my rear is my greatest foe. The 'money power' will endeavor to prolong its reign by working upon the prejudices of the people until the wealth is aggregated in the hands of a few and the Republic is destroyed." President Abraham Lincoln

It makes me wonder, was Lincoln shot for his views on the banks? Almost 100 years later President Kennedy had similar things to say and he got shot too! Absolute power corrupts absolutely. Decide for yourself.

I find it interesting that in 1913 when the Central Bank was created, we also enacted the Income Tax Law that would allow our government to take from our labor to pay for it.

"Every effort has been made by the Federal Reserve Bank to conceal its power. But the truth is, the Federal Reserve Board has usurped the government of the United States. It controls everything here; and it controls our foreign relations. It makes or breaks governments at will. No man, and no body of men, is more entrenched in power than the arrogant credit monopoly which operates the Federal Reserve Board

and Federal Reserve Banks. These evildoers have robbed the country of more than enough money to pay off the national debt. What the National Government has permitted the Federal Reserve Board to steal from the people should be returned to the people. The people have a valid claim against the Federal Reserve Board and the Federal Reserve Banks. If that claim is enforced, Americans will not need to stand in bread lines. Homes will be saved. Families will be kept... the Federal Reserve Act should be repealed; and the Federal Reserve Banks, having violated their charters, should be liquidated immediately. Faithless government officers who have violated their oaths of office should be impeached and brought to trial." Rep. Louis T. McFadden, U.S. Congress June 15, 1934.

In James 5:1 – 6 we are warned against letting money have us. Then in versus 7 – 8, we are told to establish our hearts, for the coming of the Lord is at hand.

The World Economy (Chapter 4) is controlled by the Central Banks. We are already a one world global banking system so interconnected that the failure in one area will bring about the collapse of other countries like dominos. We are sure this is how the Anti-Christ will be ushered in, and it has been Mammon's battle plan all along. Heat us up like frogs in cool water until we boil to death in our complacency.

In preparation for the return of Christ, we need to "overcome the world," especially its economic system of fiat currency. For too long we have enslaved ourselves to the pursuit of what money (Babylon) can do for us, instead of relying on God's Wealth.

Ⓜ **Intoxicated with Babylon**
When Steve Gallagher wrote the book *Intoxicated with Babylon*, he struck the nerve-center of worldly economics today. Babylon is the power of Satan at work in the hearts of humanity. Babylon is the second most-mentioned city in the Bible (290 times), revealing that its spirit is the largest counter-Christian cultural influence to be battled in the earth.

As "Wall Street" refers to America's financial system, "Babylon" refers to the idolatrous, humanistic system of the world today. The Apostle Peter recognized that this influence was so great in the city of Rome that he referred to the city as "Babylon" (I Peter 5:13). Babylon is referred to as "The Mother of all Harlots" (Rev 17:5), whose influence has affected "kings," as well as all the inhabitants of the Earth (Rev 17:2). Babylon was the "capitol city" to the first four world empires to rule over the Kingdom Economics of God's people in Jerusalem.

The Origin of Babylon
Babylon's origins are described in Genesis 10, following the account of the Great Flood. Noah's sons were told to "be fruitful and multiply, and fill the earth" (Gen 9:1). Among the descendants of Ham, came a great-grandson of Noah named Nimrod, who began the Babylonian kingdom (Gen 10:9-10). The name Nimrod came from "marad", meaning "he rebelled." A vicious take-over spirit therefore prevailed as he conquered nations form Assyria to Libya, according to Alexander Hislop. Nimrod led the people to build a city "for themselves" in order to make their name great, not God's (Gen 11:4).

The Tower of Babel was intended to be a wonder in the world to display the splendor or man's abilities, not God's. A financial system designed for "us" and not God. A rebellion to Kingdom principles of Wealth, the Tower was to be built so high, that he could avoid the judgment of God again if He were to flood the Earth because of their evil deeds. I am concerned that many Christian businessmen and woman have rebelled against God's financial concepts, and derive more excitement over the world's financial system than God's Kingdom resource fullness.

Come Out of Babylon
About a decade after Nimrod's death, Abraham was born in Ur, one of the cities Nimrod built in Mesopotamia. But after 70 years in the captivity of the Babylonian financial system and strategy, God called Abraham to leave that country and go to a promised land God would reveal to him (Gen 12:1-2; Acts 7:2-3; Heb 11:8). For the next 105

years, Abraham lived in tents and refused to settle for the comfortable lifestyle in a godless culture.

Abraham then had another business decision -- to separate from Lot later in his life. He gave Lot the choice of the land and Lot chose the appearance of wealth toward Sodom. Even then, **Abraham was learning the Kingdom concept of giving** to his nephew and God blessed him exceedingly (Gen 13:14-17). Abraham left the desire for worldly wealth only to find not only the pleasure of God, but also His financial blessings. Also, while being "detoxified" from Babylonian intoxications, the Lord taught Abraham to tithe. Abram "gave a tenth of everything" he gained in his victory over Kedorlaomer and the kings with him to Melchizedek (Gen 14:17).

Fast forward to 445 B.C. God's people had been in Babylon as the nation of Israel for 70 years. Yet, when the call was given by the Lord for all those who wanted to return to Jerusalem and trust God's plan for prosperity, not even 50,000 responded. They loved living in the richest city and country on Earth. They had become addicted to Babylonian pleasures.

We have been indoctrinated with Babylonian wealth strategies designed for our bondage and destruction, yet don't seek to change because we enjoy living like kings even if it's in the devil's kingdom. Our consumer economy is based in covetousness and debt. The two Greek words translated "covet," or "covetousness" are *"epithumeo,"* meaning lust and desire. And the word, *"pleonektes,"* to be eager for more.

The United States has become a debtor nation, running up trillions in debt because of desire for more. More than 3,500 commercial messages a day, on average, scream at us to lust after more, all the time bringing ourselves and nation into deeper and deeper bondage to debt.

The Fall of Babylon

"Woe, woe, the great city Babylon, the strong city! For in one hour your judgment has come" (Rev 18:10). One day all the deception and damage done by Spiritual Babylon (Rev 17), and Financial Babylon (Rev 18) will be destroyed. In the end, we will see it for what it really is: spiritual and financial adultery (Rev 17:1-5; 8:3, 9). "Woe! Woe, O great city, all who…had become rich through her wealth! In one hour she has been brought to ruin" (Rev 18:19). Then there was another voice from heaven saying "Come out of her, my people, so that you may not share in her sins…" (Rev 18:4).

The Babylonian System is the desire to build ourselves a name with the things of the world and to go into great debt to do so. But in the end this strategy of rebellion and covetousness will be destroyed through debt and its consequences. But Daniel, even though living in Babylon, decided not to defile himself with Babylon (Dan 1:8). And even though we are all invited to join in the political and irreligious party that Belshazzar, threw, Daniel did not go. But he was summoned for help when the "handwriting on the wall" told the king: "You have been weighed on the scales and found lacking. God has numbered the days of your reign and brought it to an end" (Dan 5:27, 26). Look at the United States and world economy. The writing is on the wall; the Babylon System is coming to an end!

Overcoming Babylon

The Book of Revelation refers to those tribulation believers as "overcomers" twelve times. The Greek word *"Nikao,"* means to conquer, to get over or through something victoriously! The descriptions of rewards begin with eternal life (2:7), crowns (2:10), and white victor's stones (2:17), to power over the nations (2:26-28). The apostle Paul reminds us that we will "judge angels and the world" (I Cor 6:2-3). Christ will even allow us to sit with Him on His throne (2:21). There are over 100 prophecies related to the millennial reign of Christ. We will rule and reign with Christ (Rev 5:10), but we shall also enjoy the restoration of all things (Acts 3:20-21), forever (Isa. 9:7). God sees believers overcoming Babylon prior to the rapture of the Church and throughout the tribulation until its destruction. So operate the way the Lord wants you to operate in business; be an overcomer and learn to reign as a king and priest before God in Kingdom Economics. Ⓜ

Clearly We Need A Plan B

In Chapters 8 – 12 we will develop this "Plan B" to overcome the "captivity" of debt, navigate the "wilderness" of these end times, and "occupy the promise" God has for His Children.

Chapter 6: Kingdom Economics – By Multiplication

In Chapter 3, we discussed how God made us His Sub-Creators and has given us the right to "increase" His Wealth based on our use of Seed Faith and Multiplication. If you recall, we discovered how a single grain of wheat given enough "time" and sown into proper ground, would multiply to a field of wheat – hence the subtitle of this book "Sow A Seed – Feed A Nation."

By contrast, in Chapter 4, we learned that the World Economic System is based on "division" and can only provide a "Percentage Increase." By definition, percentage (%) typically means a fraction or less than one (<1). For example, if we earn four percent (4%) on our Assets (say $1,000), then after one year's time, we would have $1040 (see the banking example in Chapter 3). Further, the Rule of 72's then tells us that it will take 18 years for our money (resources) to double (72/4 = 18). For Kingdom purposes, that simply is just too long! Therefore, let's agree that Division or Percentage Increase doesn't work for our purposes.

Managing Your Personal Resources. In this Chapter we will look first at how we make decisions about managing our personal resources and then how we should be managing God's Wealth.

Most financial advisors would tell us to: 1) develop a personal budget or spending plan, 2) create an emergency fund to plan for unforeseen emergencies (off budget), 3) save for our dream vacations or adult toys, and 4) plan for retirement. Good advice, right? This is exactly what Americans have NOT done. We want it now! So we borrow money and so does our government (see discussions on Central Bank and fiat currency) - - we have mortgaged our future for our desires of today!

Lifestyle Desires are not our needs although most would argue that we have to have a computer, cell phone, cable TV, several pairs of shoes, work clothes, play clothes, that special weekend trip and whatever else we just think we have to have and can't live without.

As for other investments, we covered the investment pyramid in Chapter 3 and will expand more about multiplication in Chapter 9.

At this point, you should be asking, "what's new? I have heard all this stuff before and I am still in debt!" Precisely, this is Mammon's Financial Plan for you (the World Economic System). His goal is to enslave you with debt (see Chapter 5). Remember, the famous old miners' song, *"You load sixteen tons and what do you get? Another day older and deeper in debt... tell Saint Peter that I can't go; I owe my soul to the company store!"* Is this you?

So what is missing from Mammon's proven plan? **That's right, GIVING!** His plan is very self-centered and not other-centered. In fact, if Christians today actually gave 10% of their gross income, there would be more than enough funds to achieve the Great Commission, but sadly we don't. The opposite of Greed is GIVING. The difference in the two systems is buying and selling versus giving and receiving. God's ways are not Satan's ways.

God's Way. The Kingdom Economic System is quite different. For example, Jesus provides our covering (Eph 4: 3-6), else we would have division. We are called to unity (John 17). We are told to "seek ye first the Kingdom, then all these things will be added to you" (Matt 6:23).

Dr. Gordon Bradshaw, speaking at the Kingdom Economic Yearly Summit Canada (K.E.Y.S. Canada) said, "before multiplication can occur, God must first use addition with you." This means God will have to add to your works (calling or mantle) first. The Bible says, that Faith without works is Dead. As a mathematician, I had to write it in formula form:

Faith × Works = ???

> If Works < or = 0, **your Faith is DEAD**.
>
> If Works > 0, but < 1 = The World System
>
> If Works > 1 = The Kingdom System

What this really means is that God cannot entrust you with His Wealth Management until the product of your Faith and Works is greater than 1 (>1). You have to ask yourself, which system do you have Faith in – the World System or the Kingdom System? If it is the World's System, you have decided to self-limit your results by using a "fractional" system and the best you can hope for is a Percentage Increase!

Kingdom Faith.

For true Faith Multiplication, your Faith × Works must be greater than 1 (>1). God offers us much more, why not 5, 10, 30, 60 or 100 times return? Why wait 18 years for a Percentage Increase to double your investment; why not this year? Simply, we lack the Faith or lack the willingness, discipline, character and/or obedience to apply Kingdom Principles (Do the work and see the results!).

Ⓜ Before we take these ideas much further, Mark please teach our readers about potatoes...

Faith Like Potatoes

El Nino comes around every 3-7 years in South Africa. This potentially devastating weather phenomenon occurs when a warm current of water in the Eastern Pacific triggers unusual weather conditions by bringing torrential rains in some places and drought in others. In 1997, the signs of El Nino bringing severe drought to South Africa were the strongest in 50 years. The Agricultural Union had succumbed to the circumstances.

- "Don't plant expensive crops"

- "Keep your outlay to a minimum"

- "This is going to be a drought year, so it's a year to consolidate."

There was a Christian farmer by the name of Angus Buchan who dared to believe that God was greater that El Nino. "This year", he said, "we are going to plant potatoes and dried beans. We are going to trust God for our needs. To Hades with El Nino!" It would be the very first time Buchan had grown potatoes, but that year, when everyone else was in fear, Buchan's faith showed everyone that God makes the difference in business.

Peter Marshall coined the phrase, "Faith is like Potatoes – plain, simple real faith that will sustain us in our everyday lives." Kingdom Faith begins with a "Seed." In Mark 4:31-32, Jesus said the smallest seed of faith [mustard] could produce the largest results. Don't limit what God can do through you in the Kingdom.

(Ps 78:41). A Seed represents "**Potential**," but your potential must be developed. When describing the unlimited potential of "seed faith," Jesus used the greatest obstacles latent in the first-century minds to illustrate the potential of faith. By faith you can uproot trees (Luke 17:6), move mountains (Matt. 17:20), making all things possible for you (Mark 9:23).

Faith is also a "**Substance**." Potatoes have substance to them. The substance of our faith is the Word of God (Rom 10:17). But the key is what you hear and how you measure what you hear. In Mark 4:9, Jesus exhorts, "He that has ears, let him hear…" He further warns, "Be careful what you hear: with what measure you use, it will be measured back to you" (Mk 4:24). If the IRS calls you, you might measure that call as important and pay close attention to everything being said. But many times we only casually listen and regard the Word of God. If the Federal Reserve Chairman says we're going to raise loan interest rates, you might fear inflation. But you might disregard God's sovereignty over the economy as demonstrated when Isaac sowed in a famine and received a 100-fold return on his investment (Gen. 26:12).

What Have We "Bought" Into?

Let me illustrate this point with a story from Graig Grochelle's book, *The Christian Atheist.*

> *A pastor once asked his church to pray that God would shut down a neighborhood bar. The whole church gathered for an evening prayer meeting, pleading with God to rid the neighborhood of the evils of this bar. A few weeks later, lightning struck the bar and burned it to the ground.*

> *Having heard about the church's prayer crusade, the bar owner promptly sued the church. When the court date finally arrived, the bar owner passionately argued that God struck his bar with lightning because of the church member's prayers. The pastor backtracked, brushing off the accusations. He admitted the church prayed, but he also affirmed that no one in his congregation really expected anything to happen.*

> *The judge leaned back in his chair with a mix of amusement and perplexity on his face. Finally he spoke: "I can't believe what I'm hearing. Right in front of me is a bar owner who believes in the power of prayer and a pastor who doesn't."*

Jesus used the word "hear" 13 times in Mark 4. Who are you listening to? The fear-mongers who give us the news everyday or the Lord? Jesus describes the devastating effects of not hearing the Word. You can wind up with superficial faith (Mk 4: 4, 15), a shallow one (vv 5-7, 16, 17), or a stunted faith (vv 7, 18-19). Jesus rather desires that we have substance to our faith and live in the "Supernatural" (vv 8, 20).

Ⓜ   According to the Bible, God is not a respecter of persons. Said another way, God gives everyone the same relationship. In Geometry this can be defined[1] as a Circle – a closed plane curve at a given [equal] distance from a point "within" called a center (emphasis added).

God's Model is not the Babylonian Pyramid (see Chapters 4 and 5) it **is represented by three concentric circles** which are a symbol of His nature (unity). The World's System is the pyramid which by its design draws all its power to the top. The Kingdom System, spreads it evenly around. In Chapter 8, we will expand this system to include an entire governance concept called a Collaborative Commonwealth. God's Model can be expressed as Provision ➔ Overflow ➔ Multiplied Wealth.

In **the Inner Circle, is God's Provision** (Matt. 6:28) which is provided for us and we cannot earn it per se. God provides for us, because He loves us as His children (God gives and we receive).

When God's Provision, which differs from Saint to Saint according to your calling and God's timing, exceeds our personal needs, you get the **Middle Circle – God's Overflow.** From God's Overflow, He evaluates your Faith to see if you will "give" to others who need His Provision. If you manage small things (worldly things) well, then God will let you oversee big things (Kingdom Wealth) (Luke 16:10). This Change in thinking is hard. I have a friend who explains change this way, "change is like converting to the next version of Windows® - - we all resist it greatly because it makes us uncomfortable and it is an unknown outcome!" Jesus asks us to **GIVE and don't worry about the outcome.** Consider Mark 10: 17 – 27,the story of the Rich Young Ruler,

*¹⁷ As He was setting out on a journey, a man ran up to Him and knelt before Him, and asked Him, "Good Teacher, what shall I do to inherit eternal life?" ¹⁸ And Jesus said to him, "Why do you call Me good? No one is good except God alone. ¹⁹ You know the commandments, 'DO NOT MURDER, DO NOT COMMIT ADULTERY, DO NOT STEAL, DO NOT BEAR FALSE WITNESS, Do not defraud, HONOR YOUR FATHER AND MOTHER.'" ²⁰ And he said to Him, "Teacher, I have kept all these things from my youth up." ²¹ Looking at him, Jesus felt a love for him and said to him, "One thing you lack: go and sell all you possess and **GIVE** to the poor, and you will have treasure in heaven; and come, follow Me." ²² But at these words he was saddened, and he went away grieving, for he was one who owned much property.*

²³ And Jesus, looking around, said to His disciples, "How hard it will be for those who are wealthy to enter the Kingdom of God!" ²⁴ The disciples were amazed at His words. But Jesus answered again and said to them, "Children, how hard it is to enter the Kingdom of God! ²⁵ It is easier for a camel to go through the eye of a needle than for a rich man to enter the Kingdom of God." ²⁶ They were even more astonished and said to Him, "Then who can be saved?" ²⁷ Looking at them, Jesus said, "With people it is impossible, but not with God; for all things are possible with God."

Lastly, the **Outer Circle represents God's Multiplied Wealth** (which has no end). Once found faithful, you can experience the full blessings that come from managing God's Wealth and God will teach you to multiply His resources for Kingdom purposes.

A king can only rule over what he can defend. Therefore growing your business, ministry, or calling will be met with spiritual warfare (1Tim. 6:9-12 and Eph. 6:12). **One way to combat Mammon's Plan of Greed and Debt enslavement is to GIVE generously, as this simple but powerful act tells Satan that your source is God and not the World Economic System.**

Kingdom Management - Four Guiding Pillars

As I evaluated my Convergence and call to be a Kingdom Manager of Multiplied Resources, I discovered **Four Guiding Pillars** from Scripture:

I. **Principles of the Harvest** (a form of Sowing and Reaping).

    a. **Sow With a Purpose, not Chaos.** Don't be careless with your seed. In fact cherish it since every seed is valuable and its loss can have great impact on Kingdom recipients. (Remember, From A Single Seed – You Can Feed A Nation.)

    b. **Don't Scatter Your Seed Greater Than You Can Plow.** Meaning: If you sow seed into fertile plowed soil, you will receive multiplication (1 seed of corn produces 1 stalk of corn with several ears and each ear will have over 100 seeds). If you sow on hard soil it is likely that your seed (dream) will die (Matt. 13:4-8). If you cannot manage your crop, the evil one will sow tares into your harvest (Matt. 13: 24-30).

    c. **Plant More Than You Need.** Meaning: You need to know your limits and not waste the blessing of God. You must know how to determine "how much is enough for you" and then allow others (i.e. widows and orphans Lev. 19: 9-10) to glean the harvest so the blessing is multiplied. (Also see IV.)

II.　Parables of the Talents/Minas

a. In the Parable of the Talents (Matt 25: 14-30), we know there were three who received 5, 2 and 1 talents respectfully. The ones with 5 and 2 multiplied their talents (double), but the one with one talent played it safe and hid his. When God first showed me this I learned two things. First, as Christians we are playing it way too safe. We are risk adverse and God wants us to take risks and multiply; otherwise, we are hoarding God's gift for ourselves. Second, the **Church has received donations from believers, but they have not multiplied it, or even saved it; they have spent it.** If you recall from Chapter 4, LifeWay Research shows that churches today are spending most of their income on buildings and staff and only 5% goes to aid the poor in missions and evangelism. If God punished the one with one talent who buried it, what will be His punishment of the Church who misspent it?

b. In the Parable of the Minas, basically it is the same story, but we are encouraged to use business as a way to multiply. (Luke 19: 11-27)

III.　Feeding of the 5,000

The miracle that occurred on the mount (Matt. 14: 15-21) is often seen as simply Jesus feeding the hungry and while that is true, the real lesson was shown to me by God. There was a young man, a boy, who had 2 loaves and 3 fishes. In this parable, God showed me that the young man is like an entrepreneur with more than enough for himself, but not enough to feed everyone. However, he was willing to give all that he had so God could do this miracle. In the first movement, Jesus gave thanks and then broke the bread and fishes into enough pieces to feed 5,000 men and their families. Next, He took the leftovers and provided 12 baskets of pieces. **This multiplication shows that if you will allow God to work with you, He will take your resources and multiply them enough to meet the immediate need and to go forward in the future.**

IV.   Allow Gleaning of Your Fields

In this story, we see that a farmer plants a field. Come harvest time, he collects his reward for having faith in the planting of seed, overseeing his responsibility, and now getting the multiplied increase that God promised. However, he is instructed to leave the corners and the edges for the widows and orphans (the poor). **This is interesting; God allows us to keep the abundance, but He multiplies that which remains to feed those (people and creatures) who cannot grow for themselves.**

What is the lesson to learn here? I think it is simply that it is okay in your well-doing that you prosper well, but that you are to remember the source of your increase and prosperity and feed His sheep (John 21: 15-17).

We believe in developing Kingdom strategies, and these Four Guiding Pillars must be used to develop your Kingdom Plan. Remember: **Kingdom Multiplication: Sow A Seed – Feed A Nation**.

Are You Called To Be A Kingdom Manager?

If you believe you have been called by God to be a Kingdom Manager or support to such a leader, you are accountable to God for ensuring these 4 Pillars are incorporated into your Plans.

As a Kingdom Manager, you are a Sub-Creator with God. As a Sub-Creator, you are looking for God to give you the right resources that God needs multiplied to be yet multiplied again with your faith and obedience to complete His Kingdom Purpose. **Remember, it is God's Kingdom Purpose, not your business plan or purpose.** Is your source your Soul, or is it God's Spirit?

Ⓜ The Soul Train

"Soul Train" was an American musical variety show that ran from 1971 — 2006. It featured emotional performances by R & B, soul, hip hop, funk, jazz, disco, and gospel artists. It became the longest continuously-running television series in American television history: a total of 35 years!

Actually however, the spiritual soul train series has been running a lot longer. Even though Scripture declares that we are to be led by the Spirit (Rom. 8:14), many times believers are led by their own emotional soul train. The soul psyche represents our mind, will, and emotions. Instead of being led by our spirit, often we are led by our fleshly, carnal or emotional feelings in business decisions. If we are to live in health and "prosper," even as our "soul prospers" (3 John 2), then we have to hear the word of God which is able to divide soulish thoughts from our spirit (Heb. 4:12), and save our souls (James 1:21). Besides, Jesus asked, "What shall it profit a person to gain the whole world, yet lose his own soul?" (Matt 16:26).

The first step in making spiritual decisions and not "soulish" ones is becoming born again (John 3:3). Jesus told the religious Jews that they had never heard God's voice, neither did the word dwell in them (John 5:37). Again Jesus asked rhetorically," Why is my language not clear to

you? You are unable to hear what I say because your father is the devil"
(John 8:43).

**Secondly, you need to focus on hearing from the Lord in your
business decisions.** The command "to hear" occurs 201 times in the
Old Testament alone; all verb forms of "hear" occur 1,159 times in the
Bible. Thirty-one times the prophets implore us to "Hear the Word of
the Lord that your soul might live." The wise person recognizes that
hearing the Word of God is foundational to a blessed life (Matt 7:24).

Yet, sometimes God's people "stop up their ears, least they should hear"
(Zech. 7:12-13), because they want to be led by their flesh or soul, and
not God's Spirit. Sometimes believers hear from God, but rebel against
what He says (Deut. 1:43). Other times we have hard hearts (Heb. 3:7;
4:7), or turn away from hearing God (Deut. 30:17-18). But most of the
time, we have heard God's voice, yet chosen to listen to another voice
that appeals to our soul (mind, will, emotions).

Third, screen out the "soulish voices" in your life. We don't have to
look far into the Bible before finding our example of making a soulish
decision. In Genesis chapter three, Adam and Eve enjoyed a daily
conversation with God in the Garden of Eden (Gen. 3:8). Yet, Eve began
to listen to the serpent's voice who appealed to her flesh and soulish
natures. First, he tempted her to question the voice of God. "Has God
said?" (Gen. 3:1). Secondly, he tempted her to doubt the truth of God's
word (Gen. 3:4). The serpent appealed to her soul: her mind (Gen 3:1,
4), her emotions; the woman saw the tree was pleasant to the eyes and
to be desired to make her wise (3:6); and her will (Gen. 3:6…she took
the fruit and did eat). Then the Lord asks:

> **The first question the Lord asked after their sin was,
> "Where are you"** (Gen. 3:9)? Making wise, Spirit-led
> decisions always begin with our daily walk with Christ.

The second question He asked was, "Who have you been listening to" (Gen. 3:11)? Whoever you listen to, can control your life.

Ⓜ The Lord asked Elijah "What are you doing here" (I Kings 19:9)? Elijah was running for his life because he listened to Jezebel (I Kings 19:2). King Saul listen to the people (I Sam. 15:24), and Israel listened to the ten negative spies (Deut. 1:45). Soulish decisions always get us in trouble!

Four Steps To Determine Your Kingdom Purpose.

Step1. Pray and Listen for God's voice so that you can hear the Kingdom Plan and know how to properly Align His Team. If you are like me, you often have a hard time hearing with certainty God's voice.

My wife, Cheryl-Ann is called to advise marketplace leaders on how to come into agreement with God's Purpose (alignment), hear God's voice (sound), choose the proper team (rank, file and order) and minimize distractions. If you are serious about fulfilling God's Plan for your life and you have not perfected hearing from God, I strongly recommend you read her book Sound Alignment.

Since you are multiplying God's resources for His Purpose, He will see to it that during your Convergence process you will get all the training and knowledge you need (Chapter 1). God will not give you an assignment He does not equip you to complete. Here is a **quick test if you have heard from God; has He equipped you for the task or are you doing this from your head for your purposes?**

The Bible records the relationship between prophets and kings. The Lord knew that my personal bandwidth of frequencies (channels) that I could hear His voice was narrow. He sent me my wife who has been a prophet to various marketplace leaders and experienced in training them in how to *Hear God's Voice.*

My wife Cheryl-Ann is truly my help meet. She hears with very high accuracy from the Lord across multiple frequencies. Prior to leaving an advisory engagement, she would assess the leadership team on their accuracy rate on hearing God on very specific business decisions. Her expected outcome for them was a 70% or greater accuracy in hearing God's voice as to His "yes, no or wait" on these key decisions. She fully trusted that God's spirit would grow their accuracy rate much higher over time. In 2012, she plans to release a multi-hour CD program on this critical training for the body of Christ.

Wouldn't it be great that you could be certain that you knew what God's Assignments were for you, who to add to your team so that you could avoid misalignments and the cost in Time, Talent, and Treasure? **If you are a king or a Kingdom Manager, then who is your prophet or (priest)?** In the meantime, ask the Lord to provide His prophet or priest for you and your mandate. Get Cheryl-Ann's book, and find how to develop this resource for you from your community of believers. Go to www.Cheryl-Ann.com and get her DVD on *Hearing God's Voice.*

Step 2. Identify the Kingdom Resources you will need to multiply for your Kingdom Project/Calling as a Kingdom Manager. Most Kingdom projects and businesses for that matter fail for two main reasons: 1) Lack of capital, and 2) Lack of a well-thought-out business plan. In third place, is that likely your team quits out of frustration over the first two. If you know it is God's Kingdom Project and you have His Project Team assembled, He will lead you to the Kingdom Resources you require to complete your assignment. Or God will give you the contacts and resources to multiply so that you will have all you need and there is enough left over to bless yourself and others. Review the 4 Pillars again, if you don't understand how this works.

Step 3. Multiply Your Resources and Results. God will take His resources and your faith, then multiply it times your works (labor) and achieve a 30, 60, 100 fold return or more. This return will always be enough to accomplish your Kingdom Task, take care of your provision, and leave enough excess to have seed to replant and to feed the widows, orphans, infirm and those whom God wishes to bless. Make sure your Kingdom Plan incorporates all aspects of the 4 Pillars.

Step 4. A Warning – Don't Rob God – Keep Your Word! As told at the beginning of Acts Chapter 5, Ananias and Sapphira, following Barnabas' example but not willing to give all, also sold their land but withheld a portion of the sales and lied about it. Ananias presented his donation to Peter claiming that it was the entire amount from the land sale. Peter replied, "Why it is that Satan has so filled your heart that you have lied to the Holy Spirit?" Peter pointed out that Ananias was in control of the money and "could give or keep it as he saw fit" (the point here is do what you say you are going to do before God does His multiplication – don't let greed step in), but that he had withheld it from Peter and lied about it, and stated that Ananias had not only lied to Peter, but also to God. Ananias died on the spot and was carried out. As a result, everyone who heard the incident feared the Lord. Later his wife told the same lie and also fell dead.

The warning here is to be careful how you covenant with God. God wants you to be rewarded for your faithfulness as His Kingdom Manager. Once you are clear what your needs are, when the project unfolds and God does His multiplication miracle, don't change the deal and keep more back for you; it could cost you your life or your reputation! Don't work for free either and hurt your family. This is not God's way to hurt you while He helps others. He is not a respecter of persons. Every situation is unique for God's Kingdom Purpose (see Step 1). **The key is that when you covenant with God, keep your word and He will keep His!**

Use the Plan that follows as a guideline for developing your projects.

A Sample Kingdom Management Plan

Mandate: Kingdom Manager to feed the homeless in your community.

Goal: Sow A Seed – Feed A Nation (at least my community)

My Purpose: 1) To pray and seek God's Will

2) Identify my Kingdom Resources

3) Develop my Multiplication Strategy

4) Don't rob God – Keep my word!

My Plan: An Urban Organic U-Pick Farm

I. **Using the Principals of the Harvest**:

a. **Sow with a Purpose**. Feed the homeless the "best" organic fruits and vegetables we can grow.

b. **Don't scatter my seed greater than I can plow**. Using hydroponic technology and 1/3 acre of excess church property, establish my U-Pick farm.

c. **Plant more than we need**. We will plant enough for our fellowship to be able to buy the best fruits and vegetables to eat at less cost and greater quality than the grocery store and have enough left over to feed God's needy (the homeless, widows, and orphans)

II. **Parable of the Talents/Minas.** Using our Time, Talent, and Treasure, we will multiply this investment by at least double.

III. **Feed The 5,000.** Not only will we plan to feed the homeless, we will provide an above-average return on investment for those who shared their excess resources with us (bought member shares in our cooperative) in Faith.

IV. **Gleaning of the Fields.** We will meet our objective with the gleanings of the farm, using the main crops to repay our investors (members), expand our farm, and grow other area ministries by selling to the public our quality fruits and vegetables.

Chapter 7: The Fourth Sector: Cooperative

In this chapter, we will focus on the Fourth Sector of Economics, called Cooperative. When I was looking for a funding solution for Kingdom projects by using "social enterprise or earned-income strategies", I was reminded by my dear friend David Wray that I had contributed to the independent pharmacists forming a cooperative while I was on contract with the Alabama Independent Drug Store Association (AIDA). David said that in the 10 years since he had invested $1,000 in a cooperative share, that he had received more than 100 times the financial benefit. He strongly recommended that if I would consider cooperatives, the answer might be there." Truly **a Divine Word of Knowledge**.

Are you listening to those around you about your mandate? God will send others into your life to give you a gentle nudge if you will just listen! (Remember, Chapter 1: Convergence.)

History – Brotherhood Economics
Dr. Toyohiko Kagawa wrote *Brotherhood Economics* (Harpers 1936), where he postulated that the "cooperative movement" would soon overtake both capitalism and communism (socialism). He believed that the only true democratic method of economics would spring forth from "one share – one vote" as opposed to the other systems which draw power over many into the hands of a select few.

As I read his book, I was fascinated that the very thing most Americans want is opportunity and here, written after the last major financial crisis, was the answer; but because we went to war with Japan, this secret has sat basically dormant for almost 75 years!

In Kagawa's model, he proposed networks of cooperatives that would be organized into federations. These federations would provide for health care, production, marketing and transport, credit, education, utilities, and distribution. The cooperative federations would also send representatives to a Social Congress and an Industrial Congress. These congressional bodies would in turn send legislative proposals up to the legislative body. The Social Congress would send legislation on social issues while the Industrial Congress would send legislation on economic issues. This form of Economic Democracy developed by Kagawa limits small business growth and attempts to keep it in the family business. I believe that we need to form a solution very close to Dr. Kagawa's model, but one where we do not lose the individual rights afforded in a Republic, and one that provides the freedom to accomplish all that the individual can dream without being normalized by the democratic majority rule (a Babylonian strategy). To this end, in Chapter 8, I will fully expound on what I call Collaborative Commonwealth.

To my amazement, there are almost no cooperative experts in this country. **While the world is quickly seeing the advantages, America is still wrestling with the "fragile" business state called "too big to fail!" instead of embracing a new "agile" business model that would merge investors and motivated workers into a collaborative effort of economic growth.**

The model I am proposing, while similar to Dr. Kagawa's, would not place any limits or caps on individuals or businesses. My model would allow each member of a cooperative to use self control for unity sake and allow opportunity and freedom to abound, similar to a Republic or more like a Commonwealth.

How Organizations Are Evolving

Today, with all the crisis and change in the world, how an organization evolves may determine its life expectancy. Organizations are driven by mission and the desires of their stakeholders. Depending on the Sector, stakeholders take on one or more roles as employees, customers, investors, congregates donors, board members, shareholders, owners, or beneficiaries.

In rocket science, we are taught that the thing that takes you up is the thing that takes you down. What this means is that that which gave you the energy to create momentum when the energy is expended becomes dead weight and we must "*stage*" or jettison it away from the organization. Most organizations do not evolve this way and ultimately become burdened with overhead and status quo -- what I have referred to in this book as "*fragile.*"

The success of any organization is directly tied to their ability to meet the needs of the stakeholders in the current timeframe or quickly be able to adjust to it, what I can "*agile.*"

"You have to become agile, not fragile to succeed!"

Earlier we discussed how most organizations are hierarchical in structure (Babylonian Pyramids), drawing power back to a limited few at the top. Change is coming and is being driven by social and economic forces. Since organizations reflect the culture, values, priorities, and belief systems of the stakeholders, organizations must become more crowd (some would say mob) sensitive. **The globalization of commerce and speed of access to information has created the demand for an agile organic model not dependent on a fragile, controlling hierarchical leadership model.**

The spirit of entrepreneurship is very much alive. Trust in fragile, too-big-to-fail organizations is broken. Innovation, self reliance, and social media communication have changed the landscape of our economy and are moving toward more collaborative organic structures.

All the while, we move more and more to the haves and have-nots as the middle class shrinks. This is leaving billions globally with a sense of hopelessness which has led to social unrest, terrorism, and collapse of existing organizational systems and governments (e.g., the Arab Spring).

"We need to offer hope to the global stakeholders."

The average family does not replace itself in society; the family birthrate has declined to under 2 in most industrialized nations with some as low as 1.1 to 1.6. Meanwhile, by contrast the Islamic family birthrate averages 6 children. Therefore, Islamic doctrine and social structure prosper in unity of purpose (even if by control) of which one goal is to take over our way of life and the extinction of the Christian belief system. Failure for us to stop the "division" within the Christian denominations will by organic growth (multiplication) overtake us. Even evil can use multiplication.

"We must develop new organizational structures that unify and honor diversity."

The Four Sectors: Public, Private, Social and Collaborative are converging as stakeholders' demands drive affinity from necessity. Government (Public) and Non-Profits (Social) are both seeking additional revenues through "earned-income" strategies as taxes and giving are in decline.

The For Benefit Organization

Society and entrepreneurs are becoming more socially conscious and government mandates are insisting on environmental compliance and so-called social justice.

Stakeholders' needs are merging across all four sectors. The rise of the stakeholder is pulling down those pyramid structures based on central control, and refocusing influence from "the few" to "the many" (crowd or mob). We can see this every day all over the world in demonstrations. **We are being told it is social unrest, but it is a change that is coming, that to ignore would be suicide.** For- Benefit Organizations merge the social needs of the stakeholders with the business requirements to earn a profit. Non-profits that don't recognize this will likely fade from existence.

Stakeholder governance, inclusive ownership, and fair distribution of the profits (not division of wealth without effort) are among the key criteria in future organizational design.

To emphasize my point, let me share an email I received recently. It certainly is not politically sensitive, but it really makes the point of how the World System is about to collapse.

The Ant and The Grasshopper. (Old and Modern Versions) Author: Unknown

Old Version:

The ant works hard in the withering heat all summer long, building his house and laying up food for the winter.

The grasshopper thinks the ant is a fool and laughs and dances and plays all summer long. Come winter, the ant is warm and safe in his home and has food to eat. The grasshopper has no food or shelter and dies in the cold. *Moral: Be responsible for yourself; collaborate with others and live.*

Modern Version:

The ant works hard in the withering heat all summer long, building his house and laying up food for the winter.

The grasshopper thinks the ant is a fool and laughs and dances and plays all summer long. Come winter, the shivering grasshopper calls an Occupy Ant Hill and a press conference. He demands to know why the ant should be allowed to be warm and well fed while he is cold and starving – is there no social justice?!

All the major TV and radio networks show up to provide pictures to the world of the shivering grasshopper in contrast to the warm ant. America is alarmed by this stark contrast. How can this be that in a country of such wealth, this poor grasshopper is suffering so? Kermit the Frog appears on Oprah with the grasshopper and everyone cries when they sing, "It Ain't Easy Being Green." ACORN starts a demonstration shouting, "We will overcome." The President condemns the ant and blames Bush, Reagan, The Founders and even the Pope for the grasshopper's plight. Leaders in Congress proclaim loudly on C-span and Meet the Press that the ant somehow has gotten rich at the expense of the grasshopper, and overnight in this carefully orchestrated "crisis," pass laws they didn't read to tax the ant and make him "divide" his wealth with the poor grasshopper! Then they legislate that the ant should have to hire the grasshopper, and fine the ant for failing to be sensitive to the plight of those who are green. The Green Czar then gets the IRS to foreclose on the ant, take his home and let grasshoppers live there for free while this all gets sorted out.

The story ends with the ant moving out of the country. The grasshopper and his freeloading friends, now having eaten all of the ant's food and trashed his house with parties and sloth, abandon the ant's house. Spiders have now moved in selling crack, and the grasshopper dies from an overdose which he paid for from his government grasshopper reparations. Now the spiders control the once peaceful and happy yard where the ants once lived. ***Moral: "The system is going to change, just like***

Rome. Will you stop 'dividing' and learn God's way to 'multiply' before it is too late?"

Ants succeed because they multiply and they collaborate together and they prepare for the future. **Are you an ant or a grasshopper, or even worse, a spider?**

The Traditional Classical Cooperative

At first look, it would appear that the Fourth Sector cooperatives meet all the organizational demands of the For-Benefit Model; however, traditional cooperatives present some negatives.

The cornerstone of the cooperative movement is the concept of one share – one vote. This model still operates on a concept of democracy; that is, the "majority rules." This dismisses the rights of the individual. If you recall from our discussion in Chapter 4, Democracies often leave the minority (the individual) under the tyranny of the majority. In Chapter 8, we will solve this problem with the Collaborative Commonwealth. That said, let's consider the many benefits of using a collaborative or cooperative.

❑ **Education.** Cooperatives provide a common platform for learning about the topics of most interest to the group.

❑ **Reducing Costs.** Aggregated buying allows members of the cooperative to share in volume discounts only afforded large groups. Further, the cooperative can qualify for patronage rebates from manufacturers which may result in patronage refund checks to the members according to their use of the programs offered.

❑ **Multiplying Resources.** Working collaboratively and using new marketing and business structures, members of cooperatives can enjoy revenues that will support the group unity and result often in above-average returns on investment through higher yields on cash and asset growth which increases member patronage refunds.

❑ **Community.** At first hard to value, but ultimately, the joining of diverse groups into a single focus creates market strength, savings, influence and recognition of the affinity cause.

❑ **Social Purpose**. Most cooperatives are formed from a group of consumers or businesses who find that working together is better than competing with each other. This social purpose creates the unity to bind the group.

❑ **Inclusive Ownership**. Cooperatives can be structured to accomplish any legal business purpose. Owning a share of the cooperative allows you to participate in the profits of the group according to your contributions. It is not equal distribution, which is a socialist ideal. Distribution (patronage refunds) by contribution recognizes and rewards individual effort.

❑ **Stakeholder Governance**. Share Members make up the board of directors and provide oversight of the cooperative much like representatives in our government. While democratic in its application, the one vote – one share keeps a balance of power. However, the majority still rules.

❑ **Fair Compensation**. Vendors, consumers and shareholders in the cooperative work toward a fair payment and compensation for goods and services. Any profits are shared proportionately based on the contributions by individuals.

❑ **Social Responsibility**. The affinity which brought the group together is maintained by equal voting.

❑ **Transparency**. Since all members can see the books, there is full transparency and no undisclosed profit taking.

❑ **Protection of Assets**. As a for-profit organization with single tax payer status, the cooperative is free to merge, agree, collaborate, join, advocate and represent the values and needs of the group without the restrictions placed on non-profits as a group.

These represent some of the advantages and disadvantages of cooperatives. I recommend that you read about the Cooperative Movement worldwide to become informed on this topic. There are a couple of key issues. First, cooperatives have a limitation on the number of member classes which can leave the cooperative at financial risk. Second, members must support the cooperative's mission by patronage (use of) its products and services.

Types of Cooperatives

1. **Producer Cooperatives:** In this cooperative, members are engaged in production in separate enterprises. *Examples* are: farms, fishing boats, forests, artist studios, retail businesses or most any for-profit enterprise. They may buy products, services, equipment, insurance, or hire managers and sales people, market and advertise together, or operate storage or processing facilities or distribution networks. Some cooperatives process and market directly to their members' products and services while other CoOps sell directly to the public. *Examples:* Agriculture, pooling of equipment, pooling of fuel, advisory services, etc.

2. **Consumer Cooperatives:** These cooperatives are owned and governed by people who want to buy from the cooperative. Most consumer cooperatives, even if they are not as complex or heavily regulated as credit unions (described below), elect boards of directors who hire managers to run the daily operations. Consumer member-owners may serve on committees, run for a seat on the board, or take another active part in the CoOp. But as often as not, their primary involvement in their CoOp is in the consumption of its goods or services. Both the grocery

and the electric industries are tough businesses that require constant professional development. Consumers can create a cooperative to provide pretty much anything they want to buy. Their purchases may include groceries, electricity or telephone service, housing, healthcare, or—under the label of credit unions – financial services. The CoOp can be tiny or immense, a single artist's dwelling or a high rise with hundreds of apartments, a small food-buying club in a rural village or a multi-million dollar supermarket in a bustling city. They provide their members with goods and services for their personal use. *Examples:* Food, credit unions, housing, insurance co-operatives, etc.

3. **Worker Cooperatives:** These cooperatives are owned by some or all of the workers. Many worker cooperatives are fairly small and have no separate boards of directors; everyone takes a direct role in policy making and other governance functions. Depending on the start-up capital needed, they can offer workers a chance to co-own the company with very little financial investment. This is advantageous for people of modest or low incomes. They are also increasingly popular with other small groups. *Examples:* attorneys, designers, engineering firms and other professionals, fundraisers, tourism, communications, marketing, forestry, leisure, production, manufacturing, bookstores, print shops, copy centers, construction firms, homecare and daycare professionals, restaurants, bakeries, auto repair shops, and groups of artists or artisans.

4. **Worker-Shareholder Cooperatives:** These cooperatives hold partial ownership in the separate business in which the members are employed. Because of its investment in the asset (the business), the cooperative may participate in the management of the business and the workers may influence work hours and organizational structure. *Examples:* production and manufacturing, technology, etc.

5. **Credit Unions Cooperatives:** Credit unions are actually consumer-owned financial services cooperatives in which every

depositor becomes a member-owner. This is quite a difference from big international banking conglomerates with their distant millionaire investor-owners and highly paid directors who have no knowledge of or loyalty to local residents. Following the financial crisis of 2008, many people have realized that financial services provided for the benefit of consumer members rather than for profit is not only better for members, it's better for the world financial system as well. Credit unions, as with all CoOps, come in all sizes--from a single facility with a few score members to huge, multi-branch operations that cover lots of territory and employ many local people.

6. **Social Cooperatives:** This emerging type of cooperative has a social mission beyond service to its members. It may have to do with improving working conditions for immigrant women. It may provide alternative health services at affordable costs to a specific community such as the Christian mutual share health plans. Owned and governed by worker or consumer members, the CoOp also may have a non-profit social mission component. See Hybrid Cooperatives.

7. **Hybrid Cooperatives:** See section that follows.

A Vision of Change

Desiring to overcome some of the limitations of the traditional cooperatives, several states have adopted new regulations which allow multiple share classes and hybrid concepts.

Consider this scenario... in their college town, three business students get together to form a microbrewery. They have a great product formula, but no money (the current state of American entrepreneurship). They form one of these special vehicles and sell member shares of the CoOp for less than $200 per share (remember one share – one vote) and raise over $400,000 to build the microbrewery. Now the approximate 2,000 college students/CoOp members send all their friends to drink beer at their pub versus another one where they don't get the "patronage dividend." The members have hired a management company (CMC) to operate the CoOp. The CoOp members and the 30,000 college students (their friends) in this town are its best customers. Think social network/ circle.

Note: Properly-designed cooperatives can raise money by selling member shares under an exemption of the securities law. This exemption is because of "one share one vote." Therefore, if you need to raise capital (example: $50,000 and you have 100 members, then create new member share class at $500 per share), a cooperative may be just right for you. **Important to note: You cannot buy more than one share, because this would void the exemption, so make sure you determine how many members and how much money you need before you establish the share price. Remember, you are selling a "membership" share, not an "investment" share.**

In some cases, you will need a hybrid structure to accomplish the capital development. The problem is that most attorneys and accountants do not understand the over 250-year-old cooperative law and therefore cannot help you. When I did my research for Kingdom CoOp, it took many months, hiring of consultants, and paying for tax opinions, interviewing lawyers and accountants to find the right mix and expertise to use this system. **I have prepared a consulting package for those who want to learn how to use cooperatives, and those interested may request a copy at www.wdwycm.com.**

Hybrid Cooperative Concepts

Despite all the recent improvements in cooperative design and laws, new cooperative structures continue to evolve almost daily. The issues remain member patronage and capital. Cooperatives are often criticized by the traditional business community as being an inferior form of ownership and "control" for two reasons: 1) decision making by a member board, and 2) capital constraints due to poor member patronage.

This mismatch is the reason the Cooperative Movement in the US lags behind the rest of the world. A new breed of entrepreneurs who, like me, believe the advantages more than outweigh the disadvantages, are creating hybrid cooperative structures to remedy these criticisms. Like the microbrewery example earlier, new ownership structures, multiple share classes, non-member investors in CoOp assets, private-public partnerships, alliances and federations, and more innovations too numerous to provide here, are changing these traditional business opinions.

Classical cooperative ownership is grounded in use transactions rather than capital investments. Typically, membership is conditional on the purchase of one share, receiving one vote, but not a basis of any specific ownership right per se. Members regularly retain rights in control in that they can elect the board of directors and own rights in residual claims should the cooperative cease to operate. As stated before, the classical cooperative distributes dividends (often referred to as Patronage Refunds) on a *pro-rata* use basis and not the performance of the cooperative as a business entity. The cooperative may be doing well (or not) as a business structure, but the dividend is only determined based on usage in the price one receives from a member of a marketing cooperative or the purchase made by a member.

Focusing on the Marketplace

Since cooperatives are the intersection of producers and consumers, other CoOps may likely engage similar strategies, but using producers and consumers we can get the idea across and stay within the scope of this book, which is multiplying resources primarily for Kingdom purposes.

Earlier in this chapter we discussed the microbrewery model. In that example, capital was raised to construct a retail pub with a microbrewery. If you open your mind, this example could be almost any kind of business! The three college students had a social relationship in that they were students in a university with thousands of beer consumers.

They had a product they wanted to sell primarily to this social network/circle. Of course they had no money for capital investment.

Their approach of selling member shares of a modern cooperative design was not all that revolutionary, but it was effective. Today, they have a great location, over 2,000 share members and thousands of their friends as customers. They have hired expert management, the model works, and is debt free. Let's start by looking at that design and then expand from here.

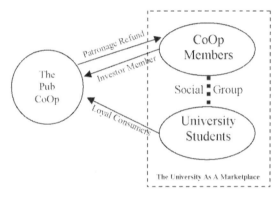

In this example, the CoOp Members are the 2,000 students (a subset of the University marketplace who bought a share of The Pub CoOp for less than $200 as investor members). They provided the capital that these broke students needed. The University Students are the Social Network/Circle and are the Loyal Consumers of the microbrewery. When The Pub CoOp makes a profit, the CoOp Members will receive a Patronage Refund (like a dividend) plus the principal invested (the capital). The challenge here is how you allocate the patronage. I would recommend that each of the 200 CoOp Members enroll University Students as another class of non-share members. This membership drive would determine the Patronage Refund *pro-rata* on the basis of members enrolled. You could have the consumers receive a Patronage Refund too (if you created another "share" class of members); it would just have to be planned out.

Hybrid 2 Management and Non-Member Investment
In this example, we stayed with The Pub CoOp so that you could see the changes. This time, the investment came from the private investor who has entered into a joint venture with The Pub CoOp and is using a

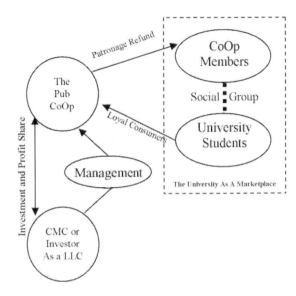

Third-Party Management company to oversee the operation. In this case, likely this manager would have experience in the operation of a pub.

Next, notice that in this example, Profit Share goes to the investor, but Patronage Refund goes to the CoOp Members (students) that have joined from the social network/circle: the University. The flows have changed slightly, but the concept is still a cooperative. In Chapter 9, we will explain the CMC (Concept Management Company) strategy. Looking next at Hybrid 3, we will replace the private investor with a public company.

Hybrid 3 Public versus Private Investors.

In this model, we decided to take advantage of the leverage that can be accomplished with a public company to raise capital. While The Pub CoOp likely would not need such an addition for one location, if the board wanted several locations this might be more than a small group of students as private investors could afford or raise.

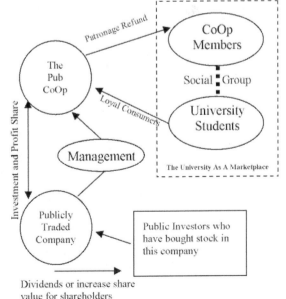

The public company has sold stock to its investors and has now entered into an agreement with The Pub CoOp to either: 1) invest in possibly the preferred shares of the cooperative or 2) purchase a special share class for which the public company will receive profit share.

In this case, the shareholders of the public company may receive a dividend from their public shares or more likely will enjoy the appreciation of the public company shares in the market. Either way, public companies have been excellent at raising capital for worthwhile projects.

A word of caution. Using a public company is inviting potential Babylonian thinking to influence your structure. Think alignment. Careful drafting of all agreements is necessary to ensure proper Kingdom alignment.

Further, some CoOps have become publicly-traded companies. While this affords tremendous leverage, it may violate the original intent of the CoOp structure. The good thing is that members got to decide their future.

There are too many Hybrid potentials to discuss here, so if you are thinking you want to create a Hybrid Cooperative, please contact Dr. Needham at **www.wdwycm.com**.

Chapter 8: Collaborative Commonwealth

A Transition Plan B: Today to the Millennial Kingdom.
In a few years, unless the Lord tarries, the World System will surrender to the sovereign order of the Theocracy of Jesus Christ as Lord of lords and King of kings. In the Millennial Kingdom, governance will be interpreted by a system of kings and priests who will rule and reign by "serving" Kingdom citizens which are the victorious remnant of the failed World System (Gen. 1:26-28 and 2:15-17, Luke 10:19 and 19:11-13, Matt. 28:18-20, Rev. 1:5-6, 3:21 and 20:4-6). [See Background on Remnant that follows.]

In Matthew 5:5 we are taught "the meek shall inherit the earth." Patterned after Jesus, the meek, by their humble, other-centered witness, shall be exalted (Matt. 23:12 and Prov. 29:23).

Who Is Plan B For? Answer: A Remnant
While there is much debate:

- Who will be raptured, if any, and when?

- Who will survive the Great Tribulation and enter the Millennial Kingdom?

- Will all who call themselves believers be "known" by Jesus? (Matt 7:22)

- The 144,000 set apart in Revelation 7:9 will witness to who?

- When we say "remnant," just who are we referring to?

Many of these questions are outside the scope of this book, but do cause many Christians to think about the end times. We have chosen to discuss the remnant question.

Background on the Remnant
In the history of Israel, a remnant may be considered a "spiritual Israel." In Elijah's time (1 Kings 19:18), it was those who did not bow to Baal. In Isaiah's time (Isa 1:9), it was those who were the "Godly" survivors. Others like Esther, Ezekiel, and Daniel would also consider survivors as a remnant. After the Babylonian captivity, there was a remnant (see Nehemiah). In Luke 2:38, Anna was a representative of a remnant in her time. In Romans 11: 1-5, Paul refers to the 7000 who did not bow to Baal, saying in his time there is a remnant by grace. During the Great Tribulation, in Matthew 25:31-46 and Joel 13:1-2, Jesus separates the sheep and the goats (*ta ethna* – nations or gentiles), the surviving Jews (Ezek 20:33-43), the remnant of Edom (*Arabs* – Amos 9: 11-12), and in Revelation 7: 3-8, we have the "sealed" Israelites. Most Bible scholars we read agree many Gentiles will be saved by the witness of the 144,000. Many may be martyred (Rev. 6: 9-11), but likely not all will be. In Zechariah Chapters 12 – 14, the prophecy of the end time remnant Jews is told. In Zephaniah 3: 8-20, many scholars believe this covers the restoration of the remnant of Gentiles (v 9-10 "Peoples") and the Jews (v 11-20). And finally, we believe there is clear evidence that people will be saved during the Great Tribulation period (Rev. 6:9-11; 7:3-8, 13-14; 13:10; 14: 1-5, 12-13; and 16:15). These together with the raptured church will reign with Christ over His Kingdom Economic System.

In Chapter 12, we will discuss "Occupy the Promise," but for now our discussion of a Plan B is about the remnant that will go through the Great Tribulation and enter the Promised Land. Logic would dictate not all are saved at that time. Our goal is we recognize the view of the Great Commission as equipping not only the saints, but this remnant as well. This means our job is to reform societal thinking by making disciples of "nations" to "come out" of Babylonian thinking and change to Kingdom thinking. Will you rise to this call?

The Basics of Governance

According to William Bojan, Founder and CEO of Integrated Governance Solutions (IGS), governance is a critical aspect of living our lives and leading others. There are many dimensions from which governance can be viewed and carried out. For the purposes of this brief overview, we will focus on the governance of marketplace institutions, but will touch on the underlying biblical truths that impact the governance of all institutions.

Let's begin with a simple definition of governance. The term governance is derived from the Latin *"gubernare,"* meaning "to steer or navigate." In regard to the institutions through which we live our lives, be it institutions of family, Church, marketplace, nonprofits, academia or government, **governance pertains to how those placed in a stewardship role are steering or navigating the institutions they lead – either in the right direction (one consistent with God's Divine Plan), or in the wrong direction (leading to pain and destruction)**.

The governance of an institution involves a complex ecosystem. Like any other ecosystem, the different elements and dimensions of the ecosystem must be understood and kept in reasonable balance for the ecosystem to remain healthy and vibrant. In an institutional ecosystem, the three dimensions are as follows: 1) A dimension responsible for policies and oversight; 2) A dimension responsible for execution and results; and 3) A dimension responsible for independent monitoring and assessment (with no responsibilities for policies and oversight, or execution and results).

In a business or other marketplace institution, these dimensions are typically fulfilled by a board of directors, a management team, and a monitoring system. If these dimensions are in proper balance, the institutional ecosystem can effectively serve the key stakeholders and also achieve the common good. If these dimensions fall out of balance (as has increasingly been the case in the American marketplace for several decades), the ecosystem becomes unhealthy and even self-destructive.

In a healthy governance ecosystem of a marketplace institution, there is a healthy balance of power, authority, and responsibility between the three key dimensions of the governance ecosystem. **The board of directors plays four key oversight roles:** 1) Governance Policy Setting, 2) Strategy Oversight, 3) Management Performance Oversight, and 4) Governance Oversight. Ideally, the board is made up of individuals who are independent from management with expertise necessary for the proper navigation of the organization.

The management team plays four key execution roles: 1) Keeping the focus on the mission, vision and values of the organization, 2) strategy setting, 3) execution of the strategy, and 4) putting appropriate controls in place to safeguard the organization.

The monitoring system, an often misunderstood, overlooked and undervalued dimension of the governance ecosystem, plays four key monitoring roles: 1) Ensuring ethical behavior, 2) ensuring sustainable/socially-responsible activities, 3) ensuring the management of key risks, and 4) ensuring appropriate compliance with laws, regulations, and internal controls. Each area must execute with excellence their given focus, but the key to an effective monitoring system is to achieve integration of these four monitoring disciplines. Much of the current practice today has these four roles functioning in disconnected silos.

It is the job of these three governance dimensions to serve the best interests of the institutional stakeholders. An appropriate view of such stakeholders in the marketplace are those parties that play a part and have a stake in the success of the enterprise to achieve its mission, serve its stakeholders, and deliver a fair return to its owners and investors. At a minimum, such stakeholders should include customers, suppliers, distributors, investors, employees, owners, local communities, and external oversight bodies.

Let's now examine this marketplace governance framework from a Trinitarian Kingdom view. God Himself showed us the perfect way to govern – based on the three dimensions of the Trinity. Our Father sets the Law (policies) and provides the oversight (much like a good board of directors). Jesus leads the way and executes the Law in a way that is consistent with the Father's will and intent (much like a good management team). The Holy Spirit is the advocate and teacher, ensuring we have all we need in place to execute our call like Jesus did, keeping us on the narrow path and providing "red flags" when our execution gets out of alignment with the Father's will (much like a good monitoring system).

When we govern according to God's perfect design and keep these three dimensions in balance, it operates based on trust, relationships, and inter-dependency. This is a "creation" operating model that produces abundance [multiplication]. When we govern according to the world's corrupt design and allow these three dimensions to get out of balance, it operates based on fear, mistrust, and unilateral power. This is a "consumptive" operating model that produces scarcity [division].

The founding fathers of the United States of America let divine inspiration and biblical teaching guide how they established the governance structure of the new Republic. It is believed that they were inspired by Isaiah 33:22, which reads, "for the Lord is our judge, the Lord is our lawgiver, the Lord is our king; he it is who will save us." The Legislative branch creates the law (lawgiver), the executive branch executes the law (king), and the judicial ensures that the law is being properly followed (judge). An important note to this – something the founding fathers had a deep grasp of – is that only God can be all three: lawgiver, king and judge. Human beings, in our natural weaknesses and tendencies, can only be trustworthy with the power of one of these dimensions at a time. Even then, we can perform this well only if we are intimately connected to God; otherwise, we struggle to even do one well. **In many of today's marketplace institutions, the power and authority of "lawgiver," "king" and "judge" reside in too few hands – sometimes for all practical purposes, with only one individual.**

An organization will serve God's people when the board (policies and oversight role), management (execution and results role) and the monitoring system (monitoring and assessment role) have the proper checks and balances in place to achieve their given roles. The stakeholders are then more likely to be in congruence with the vision, mission and values; in alignment with the strategy; and have confidence and trust that the organization is executing with integrity, stewardship, accountability, transparency – which after all, is the essence of good governance.

To learn more about IGS, Bill's team, and governance go to www. integratedgovernance.com or www.solomon365.com.

A Republic Root
In theory, a Republic offers sovereign power to the individual citizens entitled to vote with rights given from God, not from worldly governance. These citizens demand respect for their individual voice or from their elected representatives, not by mob majority or declared majority (Super Congress) which are, in all reality, a form of a Dictatorship.

As we seek change, we must be mindful of the emerging social needs which cry out from a failed global economic strategy and over-burdened families with debt distress. (2Tim. 3:1, James 5: 1-4)

Let's Review Some History
Since the time of Plato, philosophers and governmental thought leaders have wrestled with "social contract theory." Today we hear words like social justice or Occupy [fill in the blank] protests.

There are various views, ranging across all governance concepts; many of the ideals were formed in the 17th Century on how people organize themselves into a society within a working governance system. Governance is defined[1] as a method or system of government or management; the exercise of authority; control.

Philosophers such as Hugo Grotius, Thomas Hobbes, John Locke, Jean-Jacques Rousseau and Pierre-Joseph Proudhon are among many noted writers[2] on this topic. Egalitarianism as a doctrine and Social Contract Theory provide us insight into their thinking.

Egalitarianism, meaning equal, is a trend of thought that favors equality of some sort among moral agents. Emphasis is placed upon the fact that equality contains the idea of equity of quality. This means that all people should be treated the same regardless of societal diversity of race, religion, ethnicity, sex, sexual orientation, political affiliation, socioeconomic status, ability or disability, and cultural heritage.

Egalitarian doctrines tend to be expressed either as political or economic.

Political can be of at least two forms: 1) equality of persons in rights, sometimes referred to as natural rights, (John Locke is considered one of the founders of this doctrine.); and 2) distributive, where the wealth (Assets) created by labor is organized and controlled in some equal manner (i.e. Socialism or Communism – Karl Marx is considered the lead advocate). Bottom line, you can view almost anything from a minimum of two perspectives (good or evil).

In Economics, Egalitarianism is a state in which equality of outcome has been structured for all the participants. Cooperatives often follow this concept where cooperatives fix prices of similar goods or services to ensure a better market price for all members.

In Christianity, the Egalitarian believes the Bible teaches that in Christ, there is neither Jew nor Greek, slave nor free, man nor woman, defining us all as equal. However, within the wide range of denominational and theological beliefs in Christianity, there are dissenting views especially dealing with the sin, not the sinner. At its foundational level, Christian thought leaders have sought to develop collaborative communities centered mostly on agriculture or trade such as the Amish, Mennonites and the Jewish *kibbutz*.

When considering organizational structure as either pyramidal or circular (reference Chapter 6), an interpretation of Scripture suggests that Jesus spoke against hierarchy in Christian relationships:

> *"You know that the rulers of the Gentiles lord it over them, and their high officials exercise authority over them. Not so with you!"* Matthew 20:25–28 and Luke 22:24-27.

The idea of "lord over" and "exercise authority" speaks to the Babylonian fragile World System we discussed earlier. We believe as we look further into various theories, ideologies, structures and doctrines, we will discover how Jesus wants us to Occupy the Promise (Chapter 12) until His soon return and establishment of His governance.

Social Contract Theory

Social Contract Theory is the broad class of theories that attempt to explain the ways that people form governmental authority, and maintain social order (governance).

Thomas Hobbes, in his book *The Leviathan,* (circa 1660), argues that the social contract should be ruled by an absolute sovereign. Further, he concluded that there are three (3) sovereign forms (forms of representation) of Commonwealth, including: 1) monarchy, 2) democracy, and 3) aristocracy. However, Hobbes also believed in censorship of the press and other restrictions on free speech. Further, in discussing Christian Commonwealths, Hobbes justified his beliefs that a sovereign should be civil, since man has revealed that which God has said (and we cannot be assured of any modern-day prophets). Hobbes continued by asking, by what authority do men align themselves one unto another, if there is not certainty of God in the revelation? This is his justification for civil (monarchy, democracy, or aristocracy) sovereigns as opposed to a divine sovereign.

Consider this commentary by Hobbes from *The Leviathan,* Chapter 26 from which I drew my conclusions; it will help you get a feel for how these philosophers wrote about such things:

"Now I deduce from it this that followeth.

1. The legislator in all Commonwealths is only the sovereign, be he one man, as in a monarchy, or one assembly of men, as in a democracy or aristocracy. For the legislator is he that maketh the law. And the Commonwealth only prescribes and commandeth the observation of those rules which we call law: therefore the Commonwealth is the legislator. But the Commonwealth is no person, nor has capacity to do anything but by the representative, that is, the sovereign; and therefore the sovereign is the sole legislator. For the same reason, none can abrogate a law made, but the sovereign, because a law is not abrogated but by another law that forbiddeth it to be put in execution.

2. The sovereign of a Commonwealth, be it an assembly or one man, is not subject to the civil laws. For having power to make and repeal laws, he may, when he pleaseth, free himself from that subjection by repealing those laws that trouble him, and making of new; and consequently he was free before. For he is free that can be free when he will: nor is it possible for any person to be bound to himself, because he that can bind can release; and therefore he that is bound to himself only is not bound...

    ... Divine positive laws (for natural laws, being eternal and universal, are all divine) are those which, being the commandments of God, not from all eternity, nor universally addressed to all men, but only to a certain people or to certain persons, are declared for such by those whom God hath authorized to declare them. But this authority of man to declare what be these positive of God, how can it be known? God may command a man, by a supernatural way, to deliver laws to other men [a prophet or prophesies emphasis added]. But because it is of the essence of law that he who is to be obliged be assured of the authority of him that declareth it, which we cannot naturally take notice to be from God, how can a man without supernatural revelations be assured of the revelation received by the declarer? And how can he be bound to obey bound to obey them? For the first question, how a man can be assured of the revelation of another without a revelation particularly to himself, it is evidently impossible: for though a man may be induced to believe such revelation, from the miracles they see him do, or from seeing the extraordinary sanctity of his life, or from seeing the extraordinary wisdom, or extraordinary felicity of his actions, all which are marks of God's extraordinary favor; yet they are not assured evidences of special revelation. Miracles are marvelous works; but that which is marvelous to one may not be so to another. Sanctity may be feigned; and the visible felicities of this world are most often the work of God by natural and ordinary causes. And therefore no man can infallibly know by natural reason that another has had a supernatural revelation of God's will but only a belief; every one, as the signs thereof shall appear greater or lesser, a firmer or a weaker belief. ”

Therefore, it is easy to see that Hobbes could never accept a coming Theocracy of Jesus Christ.

By contrast, Jean-Jacques Rousseau went away from traditional representative governance to a more direct democracy whereby individuals vote directly on the issues versus a representative form of social contract. This ideal of "popular sovereignty" derives legitimacy by the state only if created and sustained by the will and consent of the people - - this is generally thought of as a form of Republicanism.

Ben Franklin said, "In free governments, the rulers are the servants and the people are their superiors and sovereigns." What happened to this ideal in the 21st Century? Today, the government makes rules in the middle of the night that they have not even read and expect us to "fear" non-compliance as a society.

Rousseau also believed that individual representation was "indivisible" and "inalienable" - - meaning the right to private judgment based on one's moral stand grounded in one's religious beliefs was sovereign.

Under social contract, these inalienable rights are rights that cannot be surrendered by citizens under civil sovereignty. Only when ceded or suspended, can a government act with legal rights and authority; but surely no reasonable person by act of omission, commission, or submission would give up free agency and enslave himself by releasing his God-given rights. In the 1950's and before, I might have believed that, but as I wrote in *Wealth 3.0*, citizens want "someone to watch over them." They want government to render services and take care of their needs, so they cannot concern themselves with the big stuff; they just want to play on their I-Pads, I-Pods and cell phones!

These concepts "converged" in the mind of Thomas Jefferson and others in drafting *The Declaration of Independence*. These patriots believed that any social contract that would compromise the inalienable rights would *de facto* be void and non-binding on any citizen. I believe this is why they condensed all these concepts into: "We hold these truths to be self-evident, that all men are created equal, that they are endowed by their Creator with certain inalienable rights to life, liberty and the pursuit of happiness."

What is confusing about these words: truths, self-evident, all men, created equal, endowed by their Creator, inalienable rights, life, liberty, and pursuit of happiness? Why have we brokered these rights away for a false sense of security "in someone to watch over us?" It is because far too many of our citizens and residents don't stand for anything, except for our own selfish needs and desires, parochial or familial loyalties, and warped cultural values.

By the mid-1800, Pierre-Joseph Proudhon wrote about "individual sovereignty" as the appropriate social contract. Simply stated, individuals, by themselves, can refrain from coercion and governing each other by making social contract man-to-man. **Translating this to a business environment, where governance is important, and there is commerce and exchange between producers and consumers, they relate through commerce, but they do not attempt to govern each other. Instead, they operate by contract (covenant or agreement) where all parties can reach "mutual assent" on how the relationship will be achieved.**

Collaborative Commonwealth – A New Form Of Governance
We believe that as we "Occupy the Earth" awaiting the return of the sovereign Lord, we need to separate ourselves, not by seceding from our current governmental structure, which would be deemed radical or possibly even treasonous, by some governments, but by establishing a form of commerce that does not violate the rules (order) of the current World System (render unto Cesar what is Caesar's), but rather also follows Kingdom Economic principles and governance (render unto God what is God's).

According to the International Cooperative Association (ICA), a cooperative is "an autonomous association of persons united voluntarily to meet their common economic, social, and cultural needs and aspirations through jointly-owned and democratically- controlled enterprise." Most historians agree that cooperatives have existed as far back as individuals have found a need to act in a mutual benefit relationship.

Native Americans were basically organized as cooperatives in a tribe. **We believe that a properly structured cooperative provides the appropriate governance structure, provided it is operated as a Commonwealth with individual representation, not one of the civil forms as in Hobbes,** *The Leviathan.* There are several states that have created modern forms of cooperatives that enable groups of individuals to legally as members of a mutual beneficial group in a variety of structures (see Chapter 7).

There are four states that operate as Commonwealths within the United States and as such, **Commonwealths are recognized as a legal form of governance** which existed before joining the United States; they are: Kentucky, Massachusetts, Pennsylvania, and Virginia. In Chapter 7, and earlier, we discussed that Cooperatives have been around for a long time (pre-dating the U.S.).

A Hybrid of the social contracts is required to provide an effective Kingdom social contract, and some suggested features are:

❑ The World System must surrender to the sovereign order of the Theocracy of Jesus Christ as Lord of lords and King of kings (Rev. 19:16).

❑ In the Millennial Kingdom, governance will be interpreted by a system of kings and priest who will rule and reign by serving Kingdom citizens which are the victorious remnant of the failed World System – Needham, et al, and Zephaniah 3:18-20.

❑ Egalitarianism is a state in which equality of outcome has been structured for all the participants. Cooperatives often follow this concept where cooperatives fix prices of similar goods or services to ensure a better market price for all members – IGA, NCBA, basics of collaboration.

❑ Direct democracy, whereby individuals vote directly on the issues versus a representative form – Rousseau.

❑ The rulers [managers/operators] are the servants and the people are their superiors and sovereigns – Benjamin Franklin.

❑ "Indivisible" and "inalienable" - - meaning the right of private judgment based on one's moral stand grounded in one's religious beliefs – Rousseau.

❑ These inalienable rights are rights that cannot be surrendered by citizens under civil sovereignty – Rousseau and our Nation's founders.

❑ Any social contract that would compromise the inalienable rights would *de facto* be void and non-binding on any citizen [member] – Thomas Jefferson

❑ Individuals, by themselves, can refrain from coercion and governing each other by making social contract man-to-man – Proudhon

❑ Operate by contract (covenant or agreement) where all parties can reach "mutual assent" on how the relationship [goals] will be achieved – Needham, et al

❑ An autonomous association of persons united voluntarily to meet their common economic, social, and cultural needs and aspirations through jointly- owned and [individually] democratically-controlled enterprise – ICA

❑ Commonwealths are recognized as a legal form of governance – 4 US State governments.

❑ We believe that a properly-structured cooperative provides the appropriate governance structure, provided it is operated as a Commonwealth with individual representation, not one of the civil forms as in Hobbes, *The Leviathan*. Needham, et al.

There are several economic constraints we will place on these structures such that they capture the power of God's multiplication (see Chapter 6) when we develop our strategies in Chapter 9.

Reformation, not Revolution

Remember, we are not promoting secession from the United States or any other government (a revolution); rather we propose reformation (see Chapter 12). Remember, Jesus said, "Render unto Cesar what is Cesar's and to God what is God's." What we are proposing is that we develop small agile business structures that utilize Kingdom Economic principles and governance, that will be used initially to evangelize and ultimately to feed, and care for the lost and saved alike until the Millennial reign. We recently read prophecy from The Apostolic Council of Prophetic Elders (APCE) Word of the Lord for 2012; which can be viewed at www.generals.org, that we believe confirms our position that properly structured "agile" Collaborative Commonwealths will replace inferior "fragile" 20th Century business concepts. Furthermore, governance models that are built on Babylonian structures and Mammon's World Economic System concepts (of power, control, and enslaving humans with debt and regulation) will soon fail and are destined for destruction.

Impact of Social Networks (Circles)

As we ended the first decade of the 21st Century, social media has become a means by which individuals network and collaborate on a wide variety of topics. For example, LinkedIn is a social network of professionals. LinkedIn officially launched on May 5, 2003. At the end of the first month in operation, LinkedIn had a total of 4,500 members in the network. As of September 30, 2011 (the end of the third quarter), professionals are signing up to join LinkedIn at a rate that is faster than two new members per second. As of November 3, 2011, LinkedIn operates the world's largest professional network on the Internet with more than 135 million members in over 200 countries and territories. In 8.5 years, from 4,500 to over 135 million. This is called viral growth.

Facebook launched from a university dorm room in February 2004, and reached One Million users by year end and as of July 2011 were reporting members now exceeding 800 Million in all countries. This is almost three times the U.S. population.

At the end of 2010 according to InSites Consulting, 72% of the entire Internet user population worldwide is a member of at least one social network (Circle). According to Internet World stats there are over 2 Billion users, thus making social media networking if it were a nation at about 1.5 Billion, which is larger than the most populous nation, China, with about 1.3 Billion.

Any future aspect of global planning must consider: 1) social networks/circles, 2) electronic commerce, and 3) the multicultural aspects of this collaboration. The financial impact if somehow this group united as a consumer organization, would control not only the majority of goods and services, but could declare its own world currency.

Ⓜ Who Wants To Be A Millionaire?

Apparently, not many Christians want to be a millionaire. The original version of the U S television game show, "Who Wants To Be A Millionaire," aired on August 16, 1999, hosted by Regis Philbin. This quiz-based TV show offers a maximum prize of $1,000,000 for correctly answering a series of questions. One of the reasons the world gets richer and Christians remain poorer is because the children of this world are wiser in dealing with asset accumulation. In the book, *Rich Dad, Poor Dad*, Robert Kiyosaki and Sharon Lechter point to the fact that the subject of money is generally not taught in school, it is taught in the home; and sometimes it is not taught at all.

The Lord brought his people out of the Egyptian debt mentality. He provided them handouts for their journey to the Promised Land to demonstrate His faithfulness as their provider. But He told them that they had to mature in the Promised Land economically, and that He would give them the ability to gain Wealth (Deut. 8:18). So, the day after they had eaten what the Promised Land produced, the manna stopped (Josh. 5:12). They had to go to work and learn how to produce the Wealth the Lord promised to bless them with for the sake of His Kingdom advancement. Yet many Christians today don't seek to build abundant Wealth. Instead they focus only on Scriptural warnings about money being filthy lucre and the love of which is the root of all evil (I Pet. 5:2; I Tim. 6:10). Dr C. Thomas Anderson, author of *Becoming a Millionaire God's Way*, says, "God is not going to drop abundance out of heaven. That only happens in the wilderness and it is never enough for more than the day. You have to learn the attitudes, the qualities and skills to become wealthy. For the promises of God to be effective in your life, changes need to happen inside of you."

Tithing and Giving

After a believer has become familiar with Kingdom resource fullness, ministry can benefit through tithes and offerings. Tithing predated the Law of Moses. When Abraham sent tithes on his increase to Melchizedek, he was applying this Kingdom principle. Jesus taught the people to tithe (Matt. 23:23), and Paul underscores its importance as well (I Cor. 16:20). Old Testament purposes of tithing, according to Joseph Mattera, were to…

- Support the Levites who served in the Tabernacle (Num. 18:24; I Cor. 9:14; I Tim. 5:17).

- Support aliens, the fatherless and widows (Deut. 14:29; James 1:27, I Tim. 5:3-4, and Acts 2:45).

- To build or maintain the sanctuary (Ex. 25:1-8; Num. 3:47)

These Kingdom principles were designed for a theocratic nation, irrespective of one's position or income level. This Egalitarian Model also commanded the rich to leave the edges of their field so that the poor could glean the harvest and feed themselves (Lev. 19:9-10).

Those with financial surplus were commanded to give no-interest loans to the poor (Ex. 22:25; Lev. 25:35-37). However, interest loans in general are expected business practices. In these times, loans had to expire every seven years (Deut. 15:1-2, 9-10), to prohibit the bondage of debt and the class system.

There were no welfare systems as they exist today in the U.S. Economically impoverished individuals still had to work for their benevolence by "gleaning" the fields for their food. **As we have said before, our greatest weapon against Mammon's World Economic System is GIVING which is the opposite of GREED.**

Collaborative Commonwealth Reformation Coming!
The priestly prayer of Christ in John 17, is that this body be one (John 17:11)! Some refer to this desire as the only unanswered prayer of Jesus. Notwithstanding, the heartbeat of Jesus is being fulfilled and will be fully manifested as we approach His return to Earth. Although this special unity has many last-days ramifications, I believe one of them is the return to Acts 2 financial cooperation.

> *All that believed were together, and had all things common; and sold their possessions and goods, and divided [distributed] them to all as every person had need.* Acts 2:44-45

They began a Collaborative Commonwealth system that still allowed them to acquire individual wealth (possessions and goods), yet distribute the Kingdom Wealth as needed, or as determined by equal input from the body. This is how the New Testament Church began and this is how it will finish. Let this "Reformation Begin With Us!" Ⓜ

A Quick Math Lesson

As a mathematician, I could not help it, since the name of this book is *Why Divide When You Can Multiply?*, I had to discuss multiplication and division so that we can clearly see the difference.

Multiplication is one of the four basic operations that form the foundation of arithmetic. God is the great mathematician. First, multiplication has its roots in addition; therefore, multiplication is simply repeated addition (i.e. 4 × 2 = 2+2+2+2).

Multiplication is also commutative, meaning in either order the results are the same (i.e. 4 × 2 = 2 × 4) [Clearly not hierarchical, since order does not matter].

In A × B = C, A and B are factors, where C is the product [result]. So multiplication is associative [relational], meaning if you change the factors grouping [strong × weak or weak × strong], it does not change the product [result or outcome].

Another aspect of multiplication is called arrays [social groups]. When you arrange the factors in equal rows you get an array (i.e. 3 X 6 = 6 × 3 = 18 units [people]. Finally, an area [a business market or kingdom], square or rectangle, can be defined by how the units [people] occupy the space. (Are you starting to see where this is going? If not, we will clear it all up in Chapter 12).

Quickly for now, division is the "inverse" of multiplication. Division is like repeated subtraction [taking away] (i.e. (3 × 4)/4 = 3, and 9/3 = 9-3=6-3=3-3=0, therefore 9/3 = 3.

So addition and multiplication are about "increase" [blessing] and subtraction and division are about "decrease" [cursing]. With fractions [division], if the top number (numerator) is larger than the bottom number (denominator) you get an increase. If the bottom is larger than the top, you get a fraction of what you hoped for (decrease). Maybe this is why the Bible says we are supposed to be above and not beneath, the head and not the tail. More later! I'm just getting you to think about the exponential power of God and if you recall, **Sow A Seed – Feed A Nation**.

Chapter 9: Multiplication Strategies

Throughout this book, I have expressed two items that will Change: 1) the economy and 2) governance.

Agents of this Change will take their Faith and Multiply it by their Works, while trying to avoid Distractions (the works of Satan) to obtain the Increase. Let's look at **the Equation for Increase**.

$$\text{Faith} \times (\text{Works/Distractions}) = \text{Increase}$$

At the end of Chapter 8 we had a Math Lesson, and I want to add here another concept called substitution.

$$\text{If } A = B, \text{ then, } A \times C = D \text{ is the same as } B \times C = D$$

So for this reason, we can say **Works = (Time + Talent)**.

Using substitution now we can see how to apply this equation more clearly.

$$\text{Faith} \times [(\text{Talent} + \text{Time}) / \text{Distractions}] = \text{Increase}$$

The Increase is not just limited to Assets, Currency, or Resources to get Wealth; it can be applied to projects, love, and other valuable Kingdom outcomes. It is nearly impossible to get all the Distractions out of your life, just like it is impossible to deny the effect of gravity. What we learn is how to minimize Distractions and maximize our Faith × Works component.

Remember from Chapter 8, if the number on the top is bigger than the number on the bottom of a fraction, then you get Multiplication; if not, then you get Division. **Examples: 4/2 = 2 > 1, but 4/6 < 1.** It is really about learning how to overcome the Distractions of the evil one and achieving Multiplied Faith for the Increase. Said another way, if we allow the works of Satan to be greater than the Works of the Saints, then Satan wins! The Body of Christ (the Church), you and I, have gotten lazy, wanting someone to do it for us and that is why our world is in such a mess!

Because God is no respecter of persons (Acts 10:34 and James 2: 1-13), every person receives the same measure of Faith (Romans 12:3). Jesus instructs us about the things we shall do (John 14:12), said, "Verily, verily, I say unto you, He that believeth on me, the works that I do shall he do also; and greater *works* than these shall he do; because I go unto my Father." Jesus, tells us we can do more than Him? Yes, we can do more, NOT because we are greater than Jesus, but because we can use our Time and Talent to Multiply the result. Jesus gave us the answer; we just have to act on it. Let's consider another substitution.

Works = (Time + Talent) = Calling

The Desire/Action Window
Over 25 years ago, as a part of my Convergence training, God gave me what I call the Desire/Action Window. I have used it in every business since. I believe this is critical in your self-assessment of where you stand in your commitment to doing God's Work (your Calling).

Let's expand our idea of substitution even more.

Desire = Calling.

Reading the window that follows, really take the time to evaluate yourself in how you respond to God's call on your life. Be honest, as it is critical that you don't deceive yourself.

	DESIRE	desire
ACTION	I	II
action	III	IV

ACTION = puts forth lots of action
action = fails to act, always
DESIRE = has lots of desire
desire = has lower desire

I. **Big Action + Big Desire = A Committed Saint.** You have the Desire to do what the Lord has "called" you to do and you are taking Action make it happen.

II. **Big Action + Little desire = A Mis-aligned Saint.** You are a hard worker, but you don't see the fruit of your efforts; you have not aligned your Desire (Calling) with your Action. You are letting people get you involved in the wrong ministries. It is possible you are occupying a position that should be released to someone else to allow God's perfect alignment; this would make you an A + D instead of A + d.

III. **Big Desire + Little action = A Dreamer Saint.** You talk the talk, but you don't walk the walk. You dream of doing great works in the Kingdom, but you allow many Distractions to keep you from fulfilling your Calling. Dreamers don't get things done.

IV. **Little action + Little desire = A Lazy Saint.** You likely attend church, you pray, but you wait on someone else to come up with Missional ideas and then you don't allow any time in your busy schedule to do any work. You likely don't give and if you do, you are not a cheerful giver. You have become a dim light in the world. In Kingdom terms, you have no fruit.

It is tough to evaluate yourself this way. We have learned from experience, that if you are not a Type I or Type II, you likely won't be useful in any project. If you are a Type I, we want you to determine where in this Plan B you fit and join it. If you are a Type II, we want you to take a gifting test and get with a ministry leader to equip you and properly align your gifts with your talents. When this happens, you will become a Type I.

As a ministry leader, after you have the right aligned team members, you need to consider how you can use God's resources to fund your Kingdom assignment/mandate. In August of 2010, I wrote a White Paper called, *Church 3.0 – Agile Ministry*. In this White Paper I discussed several concepts and strategies; I hope you find this excerpt of that analysis useful.

Collaborative Relational Marketplace (CRM)

*Simply stated, **"CRM meets your members where their needs are."***

In the 21ˢᵗ Century, we cannot build congregations or fund ministry the Fragile way as we have in the past. Far too many Christian churches have believed the lie that "divided we stand and united we fall!" We have focused too much on the money (Mammon) and celebrated our differences, not on what makes us Christians:

> *1) The birth, death, burial, and resurrection of our Savior Jesus Christ and*

> *2) One God – One Kingdom.*

***Collaborative.** We must learn to cooperate with all fellow Christians to accomplish the Great Commission (Matthew 28:19). We must ALL unite into one movement, yet respect our denominational and doctrinal differences by renewing our minds (Romans 12:2) to the truth of "**united we stand** and divided we fall!"*

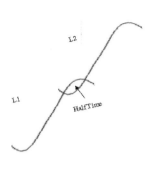

*Relational. Agile Ministry respects our history, but embraces our future. Our Great Generation, (the Baby Boomers – born 1946 to 1964) while at the end of their innovation, spending and growth phases, are also moving toward retirement. How we communicate this new agile vision to Baby Boomers will play a critical role in our success if we are to hope for their financial support. If we continue to seek their financial support, we must convey this new agile vision correctly. The Baby Boomers have already invested heavily in the big church movement and likely will resist reinvesting in this new strategy. For this reason, we are recommending the Concept Management Company (CMC) as this new way to fund this agile ministry effort. **The CMC provides a way to invest their excess resources in this new strategy and then recover their investment for their heirs!***

Recently, I had the opportunity to meet Bob Buford, the author of HalfTime, and attend a strategy session at the Buford Foundation headquarters in Dallas.

In his book, Bob speaks about a journey from Life 1 (L1) Success to Life 2 (L2) Significance as a period beginning in one's mid-40's to early-50's as "halftime" where we want to contribute to ministry.

Many Marketplace Leaders have read this book and have in their halftime gone on to do great work in the Kingdom. However, at this meeting, there were CEOs and Church Planters, trying to figure out how to work together and even though Lloyd Reeb, the author of Success to Significance was leading the conversation, there was fear about leaving their positions as CEOs.

In the book, Unlimited Partnership by Bill Wellons and Lloyd Reeb, they cite a study about what the Baby Boomers want to do in ministry or when they move from success to significance:

- *78% Desire to work with the elderly, poor, or people in need.*

- *56% are interested in health issues.*

- *55% are interested in teaching/mentoring.*

- *45% are interested in youth programs.*

Source: The New Face Of Work – MetLife Foundation/Civic Ventures

What I observed was a mental change had occurred. While these Marketplace Leaders desired to help ministry, they feared leaving the helm of their company in these uncertain times (crisis). At this meeting, I proposed that they not leave their positions, but they would offer to lend their excess to help the ministry grow.

After the meeting with Buford, I was working with Dan Cook, founder of Building God's Way, and we discussed the impact that Millennials will have in our future and the church. In fact, Dan is writing a new book about this subject too.

*In order to reach the Millennials (born between 1980 and 1995 who won't reach their financial peak until about 2025) and the generations that will follow, **we must meet them in their marketplace**.*

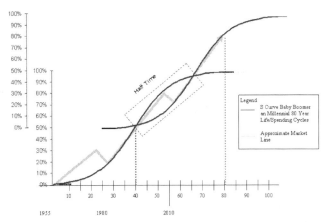

These generations rely on technology more than location to connect with one another as evidenced by the success of Facebook, Twitter, and other forms of social media.

Studying the S Curve chart below, I have plotted the 80 year multigenerational impact chart for the last of the Baby Boomers now in their mid-50's to 60's and their children the Millennials now in their early 30's. [If you recall, I used a similar chart in Chapter 4 without the "Half Time" box.]

The two S Curves represent the 40 and 80 year spending and life cycles for each of the groups. Where they overlap is halftime for the Baby Boomers. The grey line is the approximate line of market rise and fall in stock and real estate. If you recall, we had a recession/ depression in the 80's; followed by prosperity (the roaring 2000's); and now, starting in 2008, another recession or depression. This down cycle will last until 2023 according to Harry S. Dent, Jr. in his book The Great Depression Ahead – How to Prosper in the Debt Crisis of 2010-2012. This is when the Millennials reach their mid-40's and enter their halftime. This change in cycles will require the fragile church to switch to the Marketplace Church through Agile Ministry. What this really means is we can no longer build churches that don't have outreach to the Millennials.

[An outward-reaching church, not an inward- serving church]

Marketplace.*These follow-on generations (the Millennials - our future) meet in the marketplace (work, restaurants, shops, events, and outdoor activities) and not a church. They are among the most underserved in the Fragile Big Church era. In fact, if they attend a ministry function, they don't call it church, they call it "the coffee house, the basement, the furnace, etc." When they go home, they use technology like cell phones (mostly texting) and the Internet to connect. In order to grow the Kingdom and complete the Great Commission, we must meet them in their marketplace if we expect to see a Return on Ministry - ROM.*

Consider the Jesus Model vs. Today's Fragile Big Church Model.

In Jesus' time (Church 1.0), Jesus developed one small group (12) of ministry-motivated marketplace leaders of His time and took his message to the marketplace. Jesus said, "I must be about my father's business" (Luke 2:49). Jesus performed His miracles primarily where the people were (in the marketplace), not in the synagogue (the church).

By contrast, in the Church Age (Church 2.0) we turned inward, built hierarchal organizations (denominations), built big buildings, and invited the lost to "come in" and we would disciple them. This divided the Kingdom as we each found our own doctrine and way to worship God.

*Times have changed! Just as the industrial business model (Wealth 2.0) is broken, so is the Church 2.0 model. I am not saying just abandon this legacy, but we must embrace the Agile Ministry Model (Church 3.0) which will be smaller, multi-site vs. large venues, integrate technology, and meet people in the marketplace as Jesus did in Church 1.0. **We have to reach the next generation where they are – their marketplace!***

The Challenge

After spending 2000 years separating the church from the marketplace, changing back will be difficult. We now speak two different languages:

1) business (aka marketplace) and

2) church (aka ministry)

Big Church (Church 2.0) and Big Government (Wealth 2.0) don't like the marketplace, yet both rely upon its prosperity (financial success) to pay for their programs for their constituents through tithe (offerings) and taxes, but don't ask the customer (the marketplace) for input on how ministry might work. Just look where we are currently headed; government is increasing taxes and the church is struggling with reduced tithe.

Reliance on marketplace leaders to pay for, but not have their ideas accepted, has created a "hand-out" mentality (entitlements) which leads to dependence and loss of freedoms.

*Agile Ministry (Church 3.0) encourages collaboration between ministry and the marketplace. It builds relationships by offering a "hand up," not a "hand out." **It creates unity where CRM can flourish and*** *result in reduced costs and multiplied resources which increases ROM.*

Every Great Strategy Is Built Three Times

First you have to have a Vision for the Work you intend to do for the Kingdom. Next, it has to be written down so others can view it (Habakkuk 2:2), and finally it has to be built, walked out, or completed. It is easy to have a vision, a little harder to write it down, the real challenge is getting it built and the most common reason is lack of resources (money, manpower, and materials).

For the remainder of this chapter, we are going to focus on development of financial resources, since it is the number one reason plans fail. These are just suggested ways to take a new look at an old problem. **We are not providing financial, legal, or accounting advice. Always seek the advice of a licensed professional.**

Multiplication Revisited

Consider what happens when you multiply. As a commodity such as wood goes from tree, to board, to furniture, we would agree that the furniture costs more per foot than the tree.

Take a seed of a bell pepper; that seed which costs less than one cent ($.01) will in eight weeks time become a plant that produces easily 10 bell peppers that will retail for more than $1.00 per pepper or $10.00. If you look at the return on investment, you earn $9.99 in 8 weeks, which is almost 1,000% in 8 weeks. But it is better than that, because the plant may continue to make peppers all year long!

Deciding the Right Strategy for Your Vision

With the uncertainties in the capital and real estate markets, we recommend you consider, along with your advisors, the merits of using an earned-income (small business) strategy. As we discussed earlier, banks are paying from 1 to 4% (refer to Chapter 3) and other investments could be higher or lower. A properly-run business may easily earn a profit in excess of 10 to 20% or even more. Using the Rule of 72, calculate the difference that can mean for you.

Over the past 25 years working as an innovator and advisor to the financial community and as a recognized franchise expert, I learned that making the decision to invest in or to start a business requires three (3) things:

1. A Brand

2. A Proven Business System

3. A Training Program

Build, Buy, or Partner
As you decide to build a business from scratch, purchase an existing business, or partner with a franchise concept, make sure you consider the following when asking investors or collaborating members to take a risk with you.

Build. You have an idea for your own business. If you have never operated such a business, we recommend you get an advisor, consultant, or coach to help you identify all the expenses, profits and risks of start-up business. Validate your business model before you start. The SBA offers many free services at www.SBA.gov.

Buy. This is when you buy an existing business. **The advantage over a start-up is that you can look at the books and see how the business is doing.** You might consider using a Business Broker, lawyer, or accountant, to assist you in due diligence. Often it is recommended that you only purchase the assets into a new company versus inheriting the liability of the old business.

Partner. In this purchase method, you are looking to use a business system already in existence. Examples are: **network marketing** (low startup, but watch product cost), **business opportunity** (where you buy the business system and training, but do not have ongoing support or pay a royalty), and **franchise**, where you get a brand, a business system, and training. Typically, franchises offer more support and training, but you do pay a royalty for this service. My experience is that franchising usually produces the best outcome.

The chart that follows provides a matrix of nine (9) possible decisions that when you select three (3) you can get a strategic thrust for your concept.

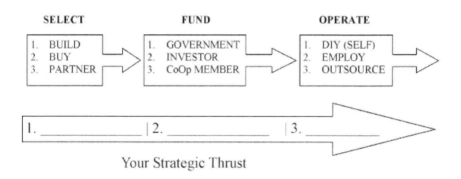

Your Strategic Thrust

Funding: Collaborate

We are convinced that cooperatives operating as a Collaborative Commonwealth are the best solutions for Kingdom funding of projects since they are consistent with the Kingdom Economic System, whereas the other three methods likely are based in the World Economic System. That said, once you SELECT a business you can place it in the cooperative and OPERATE it under the new system.

Strategy 1: KISS – Keep It Simple Saint

Whatever system or concept you choose, make sure you are suited for it. If you can't work the business, then determine if you can have someone manage it for you. (Outsource).

We have found simple ideas really work. For example, creating and selling a business directory for your church, fundraisers, and operating a thrift store.

- The **directory** requires you wanting to call on businesses and sell advertising to them.

- The **fundraiser** requires you to get a small group to sell the items for a premium price so you can net good income. We recommend only doing fundraisers that pay you at least 50%. One of the recent programs we found was hosting a Gold and Silver Buy Night where you get a local buyer to come one evening and donate 10% of the value of gold, silver, coins and collectables that are purchased from your members.

- A **thrift store** has proven to be an excellent strategy. The challenges are: 1) getting stuff donated, 2) having space to retail it, 3) hiring staff or getting volunteers, and lastly, 4) having a truck to pick stuff up. The good news is your cost of goods is zero!

Strategy 2: A Concept Management Company (CMC)
CMC's were born in 2008 as a way to solve two problems: 1) there was a shortage of money to borrow to start a business, and 2) there were very qualified people who were out of work and not wanting to go back to a job.

The idea is that you get investors who are seeking yield (often successful business people in your social network) to invest in a Limited Liability Company (LLC) and recruit talented, often unemployed people (from your same social network). These two parties come together and operate the business for a profit. We have developed several detailed strategies for how to put these programs together, often purchasing franchise concepts for under $100,000 that generate profits for the investor, income for the employees and donations toward a particular Kingdom initiative. **To learn more about CMC, go to www.wdwycm.com and download one or more of our White Papers on how to launch these strategies**.

Strategy 3: A Cooperative as a Collaborative Commonwealth.
In Chapters 7 and 8 we have discussed this concept. Here is a small example of how you can use this strategy to earn funds for your Kingdom initiative. This is one of hundreds of possibilities that we would love to discuss with you. **Visit our Groups and Blogs on www.wdwycm.com or send us an email from the website**.

Project: Urban Organic U-Pick Hydroponic Farm.

❖   In this concept, you form a cooperative of your own or work with ours (Kingdom CoOp).

❖   You recruit members to purchase share memberships. For example: your design requires an investment of $50,000. You sell 100 memberships to your CoOp for $500 each.

❖   Next you can install the hydroponic system in a very small space (as little as 4 x 20 feet) but likely not more than a 1/2 acre area). Depending on where you live, it may either be in a greenhouse or outside. Of course, greenhouses cost a bit more. These are automated systems requiring very little labor.

❖   Since, it is a U-Pick strategy, you would not put it on a roof, but that can work if land is tight.

❖   For this example, we will grow organic strawberries, which sell retail for at least $2.00 to $3.50 per pound.

❖   It will cost you about 20% for installation. So if you raised $50,000 you would have $40,000 for your system and plants. Assuming you spend about $5,000 on plants

(@ $.50 ea), you would have 10,000 plants. Remember this is a vertical system that saves a lot of space.

❖ You can expect to earn about $10 per plant, so after the system is set up and the plants are producing (which could be 4 to 6 months), in the next 12 months, you can expect to earn about $100,000 gross with net profits approaching 75 to 90%!

❖ How you declare your Patronage Refunds and reward your Share Members is key to the success of this strategy. Also, if you **Multiply this strategy using ideas from this book or from our website, in a few years time, you can earn $200,000 to $500,000 from this original contribution from your members.**

❖ **We do offer a White Paper on various systems if you are a member of our website. Join today at www. wdwycm.com since it is FREE.**

Notice. This chapter offers examples for education purposes only. The authors are not making an offer to purchase any business, business opportunity, franchise, or cooperative. You should always seek the advice of a attorney, accountant, or advisor before starting any business. Nothing contained herein, is an offer to purchase a security, real estate, or similar investment. Businesses are not risk free. With good planning, strategies similar to those discussed herein may earn more income than other investments of similar amounts invested in banks, Wall Street, or real estate. There are no guarantees of a specific result. We make no warranty of suitability, merchantability, fitness of purpose, or outcome. Any business purchase will be at your own risk.

Chapter 10: It's Too Good To Be True!

Do We Really Need Another System?
What a great question. If the "new system" was just to fix the existing World Economic System, we would say, "No." The World Economic System will collapse no matter how many changes we might propose, since it is a failed system. What we are saying is that while that system is failing, why not start parallel systems that can govern how Christians should conduct business and relationships until the Lord returns.

What happens if we do nothing? We just take the easy way out!

Scenario 1: Do Nothing!
Under this scenario, we must first believe that the system currently in place is in God's will and that our economy may:

- Recover by 2023 as per economist Harry S. Dent, Jr. Can you survive until then?

- That our Congress will become unified, not self-serving, and solve problems. What about the quote from Speaker of the House John Andrew Boehner that he, "is trying to run an organization designed to not work!" Meet The Press 12/18/2011.

- That the US will be able to repay the $15 Trillion in National Debt and not go further in debt as a nation.

- That inflation and taxes will not rise.

- That un-employment will improve.

- That the U.S. dollar will improve.

- That the failing world governments (i.e. in Europe) will not collapse and start a domino effect.

- That major U.S. Banks won't fail even though they have false asset values on their balance sheets.

- That real estate will recover to even the year 2000 values in your lifetime.

- That college students will really get the jobs and be able to pay the more than one trillion dollars in student loans.

- That pigs really can fly, there is an Easter bunny, the cow jumped over the moon, and you really look 20 years younger than your age because of all your stress.

The definition of insanity is "doing the same thing over and over again, expecting different results!" When are you going to wake up and realize that no one is going to watch over you and see that your needs are met?

Scenario 2: We Can Fix It!
This is the typical male response according to my wife. We want to fix it; it is the honorable thing to do. The real question is, "Did we break it?" If we did, then shame on us, but more likely "someone else" broke it! Will they fix it? Thus far, that option is not looking so good.

Let's assume it can be fixed for a moment. This will take unity and overcoming most of the items in Scenario 1. If everything goes perfect, it might get fixed in eleven (11) more years according to Dent. However, with the dollar stressed, and trillions more required to straighten the credit crisis, Mammon doesn't want it fixed. If our current system fails, people will be so desperate, that they will accept a single Global Economic System with one government and one currency.

Think about it, how would you respond to this offer, *"We will let the U.S. go into bankruptcy, the rest of the world for that matter, we will wipe out all the debt and make things right (remove your pain); but you will have to sign over title to all the Assets (real estate, business ownership, sovereignty, etc. and we will issue you a specific amount of the new world currency (likely electronic) and you will be FREE.* [I thought we were FREE already] *One catch, you will have to accept this mark, just a little one (likely a chip under the skin) so we can identify you as one that belongs to the new debt free system, so you can buy and sell. There are a few people who did not accept this offer and they are world criminals."*

Sound crazy? Then you come up with your own way it can be fixed.

Scenario 3: Create a Parallel System

If we can create a parallel system prior to the collapse and we can conduct commerce as Christians, in our current currency or even a private currency in the future, we can provide a way for the "remnant" to survive and move into the Millennial Kingdom.

I have used this term remnant several times, so let me be clear what it means. Remnant is defined[1] as a small remaining part. Remnant appears 540 times in the Bible. Sometimes it is referred to as the "elect." If you recall I gave you numerous Scripture references in Chapter 8.

Using strategies like those proposed in Chapter 9, organizing social circles (networks) of like thinkers, giving until it hurts, and training our youth to a more perfect way, there is hope.

Again, we are not suggesting starting a revolution to overthrow a government, since that is illegal. What we are saying is to use our God-given rights to establish a private system of commerce called a Collaborative Commonwealth.

There Is No Free Lunch!

What we are proposing is not easy; there is no magic potion, no special pill, and no instant success. We stated earlier that Faith without Works is Dead. Said another way, in order to get the full effect of God's multiplication, you have to not only "desire" change, but you have to "work," and take action for change.

Remember, Faith × Zero = Zero. No Change!

In Chapter 12, we are going to ask you to choose, to be a part of the solution or not. There cannot be any double-mindedness (James 1:6-8). In Revelation 3:16, Jesus speaking to the Church at Laodicea, said you have to be either "hot" or "cold;" lukewarm will not work. This is Satan's #1 most frequent and successful attack against Christians. The mind is a major battlefield. Satan attacks everyone in their mind more than any other way. This battle is unceasing, unrelenting and will continue as long as we live here on Earth.

> *"For though we live in the world, we do not wage war as the world does. The weapons we fight with are not the weapons of the world. On the contrary, they, have divine power to demolish strongholds. We demolish arguments and every pretension that sets itself up against the knowledge of God, and we take captive every thought to make it obedient to Christ."* **2 Corinthians 10:3-5.**

> *"Do not conform any longer to the pattern of this world, but be transformed by the renewing of your mind."* **Romans 12:2**

Even in the feeding of the 5,000, there was a cost. There had to be someone to give the loaves and fishes, before Jesus could go to the Father in Faith and ask that it be multiplied.

As a NASA rocket scientist, I had to know Newton's three laws of motion. The first law: "The velocity of a body remains constant unless the body is acted upon by an external force." This of course considers that there is no gravity. We all know that gravity will eventually cause the friction to bring the body to rest or fall (an unseen force). If we consider debt = gravity in economics, then debt will cause the system to ultimately fall. There is not a way to remove the debt, because the entire banking system is built on debt (review Chapter 5) and to remove it would collapse the monetary systems. Therefore, we can conclude that debt will never go away until the system goes away. This proof is why we can say with confidence that governmental promises and changes will not affect the outcome of the death of the World Economic System. It was designed to fail from the beginning, but only after enslaving us all.

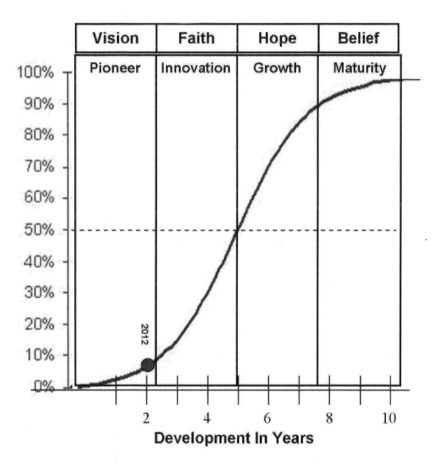

That said, **we are stuck with choosing which new system!** Wow, consider that for a moment. Whatever Satan's plan is, we know it is not good for Christians. This is why we need to unite as Christians and operate our own system.

Change always comes at a price, so that is why we are safe in saying there is no free lunch. There is no room for double mindedness; you will be forced to decide who you are aligned with, either Christ or Satan.

You will either accept the Mark of the Beast (the new plan) or you will have a Plan B (see Chapter 8). Don't be like the frog in Chapter 2 and get cooked in your warm bath believing they will watch over you. They can't fix it even if they promise they will; it is a lie.

Phases In Acceptance

Using a typical S-Curve on page 157 and a 10 year timeframe, we can see how long it might take for this Kingdom Economic System ideal to be accepted.

We began this process in January 2010 and by the time you get this book we should expect about a 10% Acceptance by the Pioneers with Vision. That means only 1 in 10 who read this book may have taken action. We don't believe that we have 10 years to implement this plan. Things are going to have to speed up.

Phase 2: Faith and Innovation should begin in early 2012. **This is where God's Multiplication can supernaturally speed up the timeline. Your Work can multiply the Faith.** If you accept the ideal of building a Kingdom Economic System and then work in your local area to build a network (a social circle of like Faith Partners), then God can use that multiplied Faith to bring the increase and shorten the timeline.

We believe in less than two (2) years time we could enter **Phase 3: Hope and Growth** and disciple between 50 and 90% of the world by 2017 or earlier. **We need you to make the commitment, and go to www.wdwycm.com today and make the covenant pledge and start your network.**

Chapter 11: Why A Federation Of Cooperatives?

As Christians and Americans we are simply too divided. This was not the intent of our Heavenly Father (John 17), nor the intent of our Founding Fathers (see Chapters 3 and 4).

In this book, we have demonstrated **the need for a Transition Plan B (see Chapter 8)** which will create a parallel system of Kingdom Economics which replaces the old technology of the "Social Contract Theory" with a new form of governance called "Collaborative Commonwealth" using the new technology of social networks (circles) to empower Christians to not depend on a failing World Economic System based in Debt.

However, to maximize the benefits of the Kingdom Economic System (God's Multiplication) over the World Economic System (Percentage Increase), we must find a way to allow individual rights, independence, and freedom while achieving the desired goal of collaboration among the remnant who will inherit the Millennial Kingdom.

The Vision: Drops, Streams, Rivers, and the Ocean
The Holy Spirit has given me a revelation of how this can work in a picture. In Chapter 1, Convergence, we explained how each one of us has been prepared for "such a time as this." **Each one of us is a unique "Drop" specially designed by our Creator.** As God placed in our DNA the Desire (Faith) to seek a relationship with Him, we feel helpless against a World System which seems to control our daily lives. It fills our minds with distractions, which often dampen our prayer life (that personal relationship with the Father). In Matthew 22:14, we know that "many are called (have the same Desire), but few are chosen (will take Action)" [Emphasis added]. We must understand the Greek here;

it is not the same meaning in English. God has called "everyone;" a subset, "few", will take Action to that call. In this parable, we learn that some of us were invited to the wedding early, but we fell away (got distracted), but now it is the time for the wedding and we need to show up, else an unintended outcome – outer darkness!

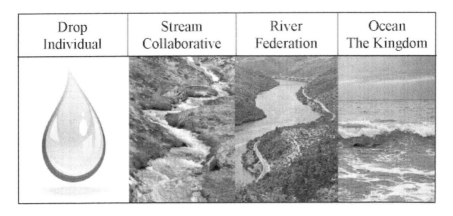

| Drop
Individual | Stream
Collaborative | River
Federation | Ocean
The Kingdom |

As Drops gather together of like calling, they form a "Stream." This speaks to the "alignment" of the Saints for their "called" purpose. In the book, *Ministry of the Saints: Rediscovering The Destiny Of Every Believer* – "Chapter 5: The Alignment of Church Government", authors Mark Hanby and Roger Roth discuss alignment and church government, saying, "The establishment of biblical government through the multiplicity of ministry is the only way in which the Spirit is free to rule His church." Further, they say that the doctrine of the Nicolaitans (the laity in control) versus the clergy lording over the people never provided the environment for God to rule His church (the Theocracy).

Religious order, not Kingdom order, has caused the church episcopal systems (not the denomination) to fall away from Kingdom order, breaking God's true desired alignment of the saints. Working collaboratively, Christians can use the governance model we have proposed (Collaborative Commonwealth) and cooperative structures to realign to Kingdom principles, roles, and responsibilities.

As these Streams merge into a River (a Federation[1]). This Federation of social networks, small niche groups, churches, denominations, and governments; each retaining its control of internal affairs, but aligned with a Kingdom purpose, become a powerful force once unified. We have believed as Christians that "divided we stand and united we fall." All the while, other groups are becoming unified, getting stronger and our majority has been relegated to a powerless minority. **The time has come in these latter days for unity and focus. We must find ways to collaborate on ideas and achieve God's call on our lives.**

It is said that eventually, all **Rivers** flow into the **Ocean (the Kingdom)**. However, earlier from Matthew 22:14, we learned that some Rivers dry up as they become contaminated with the distractions of the world. It is the heart of God that we all meet at the Ocean! The time is coming when you will have to decide and quit sitting on the fence. You cannot serve two masters; economically you must choose God or Mammon.

What is so great about a relationship with God is that even though as Drops we are now apart of an Ocean, God can reach down from Heaven and identify each Drop in the Ocean. It is personal with God.

Multiplied Kingdom Power
Drops, Streams, and Rivers are each powerful on their on but scientists agree that one of the greatest sources of power on the Earth is the Ocean. **Unity is the key to multiplied Kingdom power.**

Earlier we have proposed that we not start a revolution, because it is seen as a sudden marked change in government by overthrowing the status quo. We don't have to do that, since the World Economic System was designed to fail from the beginning; it will take care of itself.

What we are proposing is a Reformation, defined[1] as a movement designed to change the religious status quo. In the 16th Century (an interesting timeframe), Martin Luther, led a reformation against the Roman Catholic Church creating what we know today as the Protestant movement ("Protest"-ant).   Unlike, Luther, we are not accusing the church today of ecclesiastic malpractice, but it is true that division caused by church leaders such as Luther, Calvin, and Zwingli has not promoted Unity in the Body of Christ. We are saying that the modern church has become worldly, lukewarm, and hierarchal (Babylonian).

❖   **Our Reformation concept is to create a parallel economic system, allow for an individual and/or group identity, collaborate as Christians, disciple the new believers, equip the remnant for entrance into the Millennial Kingdom, and promote God's Love while not becoming enslaved to worldly systems (debt).**

Kingdom Asset Growth Concepts
In Chapter 9, we introduced the idea of using business as a parallel channel. Since the World also uses business to enslave people by drawing power into the hands of a few, we are focusing more on collaborative business concepts than build, buy, or sell concepts, although we are not discouraging your use of all four methods.

 Real Kingdom Wealth is found in natural resources such as: Agriculture, Energy, and various Raw Materials.

The idea of multiplication goes back to the Four Pillars we discussed in Chapter 6: 1) The Principle of the Harvest, 2) Parables of the Talents/ Minas, 3) Feeding of the 5,000 and 4) Allow Gleaning of the Fields.

Using the above average Gross Margins (GMs) that can be achieved using God's natural resources, we can design collaborative models with cooperative structures whereby we invest in these concepts via the share membership feature which is debt free. This enables us to keep the Cost of Goods (COG), labor, and overhead to a minimum, resulting in above average Net Margins (NM). Using the NM, we can then establish three (3) outcomes which are consistent with the Four Pillars.

Outcome 1: That the Member (investor), like the master (talents), the boy (loaves and fishes), and the farmer (gleaning), will provide their excess (assets) to the Kingdom Economic System and receive their principal investment and an above average return on investment (ROI).

Outcome 2: That when designing the collaborative concept, we will make sure that a certain percentage of the NM will be reserved for the feeding of the poor, widows, and orphans (the gleaning of the corners and edges). This may come in the form of cash, food, or other support as determined by the social network (Stream).

Outcome 3: A portion of the NM will be reinvested in expanding the original cooperative venture (multiplication ➔ God's increase). Example, if we are developing initially a 1/3 acre Urban Organic U-Pick Hydroponic Farm, we would grow it to ultimately one acre or more (space permitting). This would fulfill "Sow A Seed – Feed A Nation."

Outcome 4: Excess is used to fund other Kingdom Mandates.

The details and complexity of these Plan B's is beyond the scope of this book. **You can learn more about these multiple earned income strategies by requesting White Papers from www.wdwycm.com.** You will also be able to participate in blogs, forums, and more on this website.

As part of our research for the book, we created Kingdom CoOp which will be available for small organizations to federate and use its unlimited share class structure to birth your projects. Kingdom CoOp can act as your cooperative, consult on your strategy, and manage your patronage refund program for share members. **You will run the Project Management Company under your local name in support of building local social network branding and relationships. To learn more visit www.wdwycm.com.**

Chapter 12: Occupy The Promise

Every Great Move Of God

Every great move of God has begun with His people on their knees in prayer and with worship. Our proposed movement (Plan B – The Transition into the Millennial Kingdom) is no exception. We can develop concepts and systems, but without prayer and worship they are just foolish dreams. Every member can contribute Time, Talent and Treasure to this effort. We have said that Faith without Works is Dead! In order to receive God's multiplied favor on this journey to the next Promised Land; we start with prayer and worship. Is this your calling? **Will you be the first to start a Stream at www.wdwycm.com and lay this all important foundation?**

We are not offering some miracle water, CD on financial increase, or a quick course in prophecy. We do offer truth about the heart of God, equipping the saints and a remnant for the 5-fold ministry (Eph 4:12); and a warning not to put your faith in a dying World System, but the everlasting God. From Daniel 11:33, "those with insight will provide understanding to the many."

God has set in motion the sequence of end-time events which will usher in the Millennial Kingdom. God is NOT LOOKING for a leader or a man, as with Moses, but is activating an independent Agile collaborative body (the Drops) who will align as Streams and merge into Rivers leading a dying world to the Ocean (the next Promised Land – the Millennial Kingdom and ultimately the Eternal Kingdom). The world is moving in the other direction; it is a failing, Fragile Babylonian structure with central control and enslaves all who trust it and are deceived by it (Rev. 18:17).

According to Wallace Henley, a contributor to the *Christian Post*, "What will save the world is an 'inside-out-bottom-up' movement. It is 'bottom-up' in that it begins with the individual human being. It is 'inside-out' because such transformation begins at the core of the inner person. Truth sets us free from Babylon's bling [worldly promises], and provides the worldview and impetus for a lifestyle of responsible living that luxuriates in the joy of the liberty of Jesus Christ."

Throughout the Bible, God has used stories repeatedly as teaching road signs of His intention, glory, will, and desire for His people. Example: the younger has always risen above the older. This indicates God's order is not necessarily man's order. Traditions of men may not be the desires of God, and the lesser is exalted over the greater. God chooses to work with a broken vessel or said another way, "God builds from broken things." God will raise His Kingdom from the brokenness of the world, and the brokenness of individual vessels. In these last days, we should expect similar patterns and we will see an outpouring of miracles and power originating in small groups and individuals [Drops] (1Cor. 12:10-30).

Exodus and Exile

Be careful what you ask for in that you will be required to walk it out as part of the covenant relationship of God. The story of Moses and the Israelites is one of those repeated themes in the Bible and history. Two examples come to mind – overcoming slavery in the United States and the destruction of the Bolsheviks' revolution in Russia.

The original Exodus had three parts: 1) liberation from captivity – Egypt, 2) a journey in the wilderness, and 3) a promised land – Canaan.

This 3-Step Process has captured the minds of revolutionaries and reformers alike throughout history. Canaan has never quite been what the seekers believed it would be and in many cases was as oppressive as their former Egypt. God's ultimate Promised Land is the Eternal

Kingdom. There all of His promises will be met. At the close of this book, we propose that a similar 3-Step Process is again taking place.

Captivity

Egypt, Babylon, World Economic System, whatever you call it, captivity is a work of the evil one. God is about freedom and love. **However, we have somehow come to believe that "the only security is in captivity."** This was true of the children of Israel, in that often after leaving Egypt, they bemoaned how much better it was in Egypt.

Asking Christians to think about a Plan B will be like asking the Israelites to leave Egypt. It is hard to imagine, but at the end of the Civil War, there were slaves that wanted to stay with their masters, but that had a certain safety and familiarity to it. We certainly have gotten that way in America today wanting "someone [government] to watch over me." Debt and entitlements have their hold on us; we truly are victims of **"the fear of loss – is greater than the desire for gain."** We have to overcome this fear because only those who overcome will reign with Jesus (Revelation Chapters 2 and 3, specifically 3:21).

Wilderness

The concept of this book **to execute a Plan B and transition into the Millennial Kingdom sounds like risky business**. I call this the entrepreneurial vision. Consider Abraham (Heb. 11:8); he was the first real spiritual entrepreneur. He left the comfort of his home, went to a place he had never been, endured captivity in Egypt too, and found his blessings in the Promised Land.

Like in the movie *Mission Impossible*, "your mission should you decide to accept it…" is to leave the comfort of your current situation (in this dying world) and step out in Faith towards a Promised Land. I know some will say, "But we are going to be raptured; we don't have to worry about the end times." First, what if you are not, and second, don't be so self-centered; be other-centered. We need to be the example for those who are left behind; we need to let them see Jesus in us so they can be saved in those last days. We are concerned that certain doctrines and beliefs in the modern church have made us lazy Christians with no fruit. We cannot say for sure how God will deal with that, except Faith times Zero Works is Dead and with no Faith, there is no real belief but a possible deception – God forbid!

In these later days, it will take *Agile* special forces, highly trained and effective individuals and small groups, decentralized but united, to overcome the great oppression emerging from the failed World Economic System – called the Global (one world) Government. If we are not under one central control, but collaborate, the loss of a few (martyrs) will not defeat our cause.

Take Action with your Desires (Chapter 9), become a Drop, an element of conviction (belief), join with other like-minded believers (a Stream), unite with other Streams and become a forceful River, and lastly we will see you at the Ocean (the Millennial Kingdom).

A Better Place – The Millennial Kingdom

In Jesus Christ, we have a certain hope of eternal life and freedom from the slavery of this carnal world. Unlike Canaan, we are promised that a place with no evil shall exist for 1,000 years. This is not a sinless society, because the remnant survivors will still have a sin nature, but they will not be under satanic influence. Children will be born and it is believed some may live the entire 1,000 years. While an entire book can be written on this place and the ultimate Everlasting Kingdom, it was not our intent to discuss that here.

Our purpose was to show the fallacy of Satan's plan of Division and the hope of God's Multiplication. During Plan B and during the Millennial Kingdom, the economy will operate on God's endless, multiplied resources. The nature of animal and man will be that of peace; many believe that it will be a world like pre-Noah where it is believed that all were vegetarians. For this reason, our strategies based in agriculture are an equipping ground for this time.

Conclusions

Let's review some key points:

- **A House Divided.** At the end of 2011, we are living in the reality of the Divided States of America and a Divided Christian Community. Consider these three areas:

  - **The Debt Crisis.** The national debt has now risen over $15 Trillion and the Average American family is buried in unsecured consumer debt. The mortgage securitization crisis continues and 2012 offers even greater crisis as government short-term bonds reach maturity and variable interest rates will surely rise. Student loans continue to rise as we now exceed $1 Trillion in debt on our future workers. Is there a real possibility that a college graduate will not be enslaved for the foreseeable future?

  - **High Entitlement.** The ravenous beast called modern progressive government does not want to empower the American people; they want to enslave them, creating codependency on government entitlement programs, projects, jobs, and benefits. Control of our wages, leaving only a small portion for us, is their desire. What happened to the citizen servant? Today, government pays more and unfairly competes with the very citizenry that pay the taxes to support their plan. Bailout projects rarely accomplish anything except to create greed and failure (Solyndra over 500 Million in federal bailouts, goes bankrupt, costing over 1,100 jobs). In some cities, as children continue to have children despite ineffective government programs to the contrary, there exists often four (4) generations living in the same home and all are on government assistance (entitlements). The majority is on Social Security and most are considered disabled.

- **A Divided Congress.** According to the Speaker of the House on Meet the Press December 8, 2011, he "is trying to run an organization designed not to work!" We suspected it, but wow! We pass bills in the middle of the night no one has read and they are full of "pork" promises that we just cannot afford. Remember Tytler's quote in Chapter 4; we certainly are voting ourselves largely from the public treasury. Our Republic, which acts as a Democracy, is failing. Will the U.S. Dollar collapse? We believe it has been Mammon's plan from the beginning to enslave us and then collapse the system to form Satan's One World (Global) Government.

- **Two wise sayings**: 1) "You cannot rebuild a house while it is falling down," and 2) "It is hard to build an airplane while you are flying it." We all know that a "house divided cannot stand." We believe that America and the entire global economy will collapse; however, we cannot do anything about that, and frankly should we?!

A Necessary Reformation

Transformation, like revival, is temporary for societal change. Reformation will repair the concept, establish new governance, and introduce a God-ordained order. In short, we need a societal overhaul.

As we said in Chapter 4, pure democracy, while superior to non-democratic forms, ultimately degenerates into a dictatorship form as citizens desire "someone to watch over me." Our proposed Collaborative Commonwealth restores individual freedoms, rights, and keeps power in the hands of many while still subject to the will of God (Theocracy). A society without God at the center always deteriorates by crisis and anarchy. This Millennial Kingdom will be ordered by God's love, justice, and power. Using the Four Pillars in Chapter 6, specifically "Gleaning the Fields," will ensure those unable to care for themselves will be cared for <u>without</u> government programs.

Basically, the two commandments Jesus gave us in Matt. 22: 37- 40, should guide all that we do and say: *"37 Jesus replied: 'Love the Lord your God with all your heart and with all your soul and with all your mind. 38 This is the first and greatest commandment.' 39 And the second is like it: 'Love your neighbor as yourself.' 40 All the Law and the Prophets hang on these two commandments."* The Great Commission (Matt. 28: 16 – 20) also requires us to practice multiplication, not division: *16 Then the eleven disciples went to Galilee, to the mountain where Jesus had told them to go. 17 When they saw him, they worshiped him; but some doubted. 18 Then Jesus came to them and said, "All authority in heaven and on earth has been given to me. 19 Therefore go and make disciples of all nations, baptizing them in the name of the Father and of the Son and of the Holy Spirit, 20 and teaching them to obey everything I have commanded you. And surely I am with you always, to the very end of the age."* **This Scripture tells us how God will bring this reformation by our making disciples of the nations. One such way to disciple is to show nations how to escape the captivity of Mammon's debt.**

The changes we propose cannot occur until Christians organize under a structure of governance and purpose themselves to disciple nations to a new economic system. From the beginning, God granted us the authority *to subdue the Earth and by doing so create the necessary order* such that "thy Kingdom come on Earth as it is in Heaven."

Our solution proposes that social networks/circles (Streams) working collaboratively, similar to the Native American Tribes, with individual rights preserved (a commonwealth) could federate (join together as a river) that can "nation build" under this new social contract.

What Can We Do?
In this book:

- we have discussed what has happened in the past

- where we are now

- shown you that debt won't fix it

- shown that government is broken

- proposed using God's resources and Law of Multiplication together with Agile business concepts to capitalize a new direction that will disciple nations

- declared a new form of governance called Collaborative Commonwealth whereby individual rights and freedoms are protected and vested in "one share one vote," not a failed democratic majority (dictator) or some other failed social contract

- And finally, we need a Reformation of Christian thinking executing a Plan B in parallel to the existing but failing World System.

When successful, we will have prepared a remnant properly equipped to rebuild nations based on God's multiplication prosperity, not debt. Jesus will reign in power and love giving authority to manage the Kingdom to many, thereby breaking Satan's demonic hold, and the Babylonian System of greed and power in the hands of a few will finally be broken.

We know what we have proposed is RADICAL, but it is based in Scripture and provides sound doctrine. The economics and theology work and the governance is fair and just.

So What Keeps This From Working?

Simply You! We stated it before; when a single Drop (you) merges with other like believers forming a Stream (got in alignment) there is movement. As we combine Streams into Rivers (we get power). As these Rivers flow into the Ocean (the Kingdom) we find unity (John 17). Yet God reminds us that an Ocean is but an order of individual Drops collaborating together to be a body of living water.

This is how God established the Universe; atoms collaborated to make visible God's Creation. All was in His perfect alignment accomplishing His will. But for disobedience (original sin) which caused separation from God, it would have always been that way.

Our Challenge To You!
It is time for some decisions, so consider these points as a guide:

1. Decide to commit time to prayer about the material you have read and listen for God's voice on how you should respond.

2. Decide to be obedient to God's call on your life and find others with a similar calling and become a Stream.

3. Decide to use God's laws relating to multiplication and seek to multiply God's resources for yourself, your calling and for the poor, widows, and orphans.

4. Decide that you will disciple others such that many will be saved and that the remnant that enters the Millennial Kingdom will be equipped to collaborate as a commonwealth.

5. Decide that you will not allow any distraction, work of Satan, and lack of Faith, lack of Work, to delay or divide your taking action with your Time, Talent and Treasure.

6. Decide as your Stream moves forward to collaborate with others to form a River of power properly aligned in the proper rank and order, being humble to lead when it's your time and follow when it is not.

7. Decide if by using the ideas formed in this book, you might be willing to develop cooperative enterprises that will fund ministry and under the "Sow A Seed – Feed A Nation" ideal, multiply instead of divide God's Kingdom.

We will be adding systems to help you and they can be found at **www. wdwycm.com**.

God Bless Your Journey and we will meet you at thc Ocean!

Robert A. Needham, JD
Pastor Mark Schrade, MDiv

Chapter Study Guide

We want to thank you for your decision to read this book. We truly hope it will you assess your role in the Kingdom Economy and help equip you for your Kingdom Mandate.

Chapter 1: Convergence

- ❖ Having Desire and taking Action
- ❖ Sovereign Foundation – When God chose you.
- ❖ Early Life Development – contacts, mentors, words, ministry assignments.
- ❖ Ministry Experience – tasks, training, and experience.
- ❖ Convergence – God moves you forward with great favor.
- ❖ Afterglow – When you mentor others.
- ❖ Finding your Kingdom Purpose.
- ❖ God's Kingdom Plan for you.
- ❖ The Kingdom Process.
- ❖ Having a Kingdom Perspective.
- ❖ Assignment #1: Your Convergence Model

Chapter 2: Crisis, Chaos, Change

- ❖ Understanding Crisis – leads to decisive change.

- ❖ Assignment #1: Personal Crisis Assessment

- ❖ The Global Mortgage Crisis.

- ❖ Crisis versus Chaos.

- ❖ Change by Fear.

- ❖ Turning Points: A Pathway to Change.

- ❖ Making wise Decisions.

Chapter 3: Wealth and Freedom

- ❖ Meet Mammon: The World Economic System.

- ❖ True Wealth: The Kingdom Economic System.

- ❖ The Creator/Sub-Creator relationship.

- ❖ Percentage Increase versus Multiplication.

- ❖ Understanding Freedom – A Belief System.

- ❖ GIVING is our weapon of warfare.

- ❖ The Genesis Commission

- ❖ 3 Kingdom Laws of Sowing and Reaping
    - o You reap what you sow
    - o You reap after you sow only
    - o You reap more than you sow (with Multiplication).

Chapter 4: Worldly Economics – By Division

- ❖ Money is divisible by design.

- ❖ The P's of non-money worldly desires.

- ❖ Four Economic Sectors

  - o Public

  - o Private (Business)

  - o Social (Non-Profit)

  - o Cooperative

- ❖ The Cycles of Power: 1) Few and 2) Many

  - o Public: Governments and Governance (Few)

  - o Private: Business (Few)

  - o Social: Non-Profits (Few)

  - o Collaborative Commonwealth: Cooperative (Many)

- ❖ The 40 and 80 Year Economic Cycles.

- ❖ History – Insanity – Predictable

- ❖ The Church – Financial Crisis – Marketplace Change

Chapter 5: Debt As A Lever

- ❖ A lever is use to move heavy objects.

- ❖ Mammon has used debt to enslave us.

  - o The Central Bank – A debt concept.

  - o Impact of debt with interest… foreclosure and bankruptcy.

- ❖ Our founders warned us.

- ❖ Overcoming debt – overcoming the world!

Chapter 6: Kingdom Economics – By Multiplication

❖ Managing our resources.

❖ Managing God's resources.

❖ Faith $\times$ Works = Multiplied Faith

❖ Works explained.

❖ Satan – Babylon – Pyramid – Top-down Control

❖ God – 3 Circles – Provision – Overflow – Multiplied Wealth ➔ Freedom

❖ Kingdom Management

    o Four Pillars of Design

        ▪ Principals of the Harvest

        ▪ Parables of the Talents/Minas

        ▪ Feeding the 5,000

        ▪ Gleaning the Fields

    o Four Steps: Kingdom Purpose

        ▪ Pray and listen to God's voice (Kingdom Plan)

        ▪ Identify Kingdom Resources

        ▪ Multiply your resources and results (Increase)

        ▪ Don't rob God – Keep your word!

    o A Sample Kingdom Management Plan

❖ Avoiding soulish decisions.

❖ Collaborative Relational Marketplace (CRM)

❖ Agile Church versus the Fragile Church

❖ Jesus Model (outward) versus Big Church (inward)

❖ Visions are built three times

❖ Deciding the right strategy for your vision.

❖ Build, Buy, or Partner when starting a business.

❖ Your Strategic Thrust model

❖ Strategy 1: KISS – Keep It Simple Saint

❖ Strategy 2: The Concept Management Company (CMC)

❖ Strategy 3: A CoOp as a Collaborative Commonwealth

     o Urban Organic U-Pick Hydroponic Farm

Chapter 10: It's Too Good To Be True!

❖ Do we really need another system?

     o Scenario 1: Do Nothing!

     o Scenario 2: We Can Fix It!

     o Scenario 3: Create a parallel system

❖ There is no free lunch.

❖ Phases in acceptance.

     o Phase 1: Vision/Pioneer

     o Phase 2: Faith/Innovation

     o Phase 3: Hope/Growth

     o Phase 4: Belief/Maturity

❖ We are in Phase 2: Faith and Innovation begins in 2012!

Chapter 11: Why A Federation of Cooperatives?

- ❖ The Vision: Drops, Streams, Rivers, and the Ocean

  - o Each Drop is unique and specifically designed by the Creator for a purpose.

  - o Drops gather together with like callings/mandates to form Streams.

  - o Streams (we propose CoOps) merge into Rivers (Federations of CoOps).

  - o Rivers flow into the Ocean (Promise Land/ Heaven)

- ❖ Unity is the key to Multiplied Kingdom Power.

- ❖ Reformation: Create a parallel economic system.

- ❖ Kingdom Asset Growth Concepts:

  - o Outcome 1: Member/Investors receive a Return of their Principal (ROP) and an excellent Return on Investment (ROI)

  - o Outcome 2: A percentage of the net profit is Gleaned to feed the children, widows, and poor.

  - o Outcome 3: A percentage of the net profit is reinvested for a Multiplied Increase.

  - o Outcome 4: Excess profits are used to fund additional Kingdom Mandates in the community and globally.

Chapter 12: Occupy The Promise

- ❖ Every great move of God begins with Prayer and Worship.

- ❖ God uses repeated stories in the Bible as road signs to teach us His intention, glory, will and desire.

- ❖ Exodus and Exile – Be careful what you ask for.

❖ Exodus:

    o Part 1: Liberation from Captivity (your Egypt).

    o Part 2: A Journey in the Wilderness

    o Part 3: A Promised Land (your Canaan).

❖ Revolutionaries and Reformers have found that Canaan is never quite like they expected it to be.

❖ Captivity – Egypt, Babylon, and our World Economic System.

❖ Wilderness – Plan B: How does the remnant transition into the Millennial Kingdom?

❖ A Better Place, A Promised Land, The Millennial Kingdom.

    o 1000 years with Christ on Earth

    o Leads to the Everlasting Kingdom

❖ Conclusions:

    o We are a house divided.

        ▪ Debt Crisis

        ▪ High Entitlements

        ▪ A Divided Congress

    o You can't rebuild a house that is falling down (old system)

    o It is hard to build an airplane while flying it (a new system)

    o Reformation is necessary for social change, new governance, and a new God-ordained order.

    o God says this Reformation will come as we disciple the nations. Example: Sow A Seed – Feed A Nation!

Do you need a speaker?

Do you want **Robert A. Needham, JD** to speak to your group or event? Then contact Larry Davis at:
(623) 337-8710 or email: **ldavis@intermediapr.com**
or use the contact form at:
www.kingdomhousepublishing.com

Whether you want to purchase bulk copies of *Why Divide When You Can Multiply?* or buy another book for a friend, get it now at: **www.imprbooks.com**.

If you have a book that you would like to publish, contact Larry Davis, Publisher, at (623) 337-8710 or email: ldavis@intermediapr.com or use the contact form at: www.kingdomhousepublishing.com